Basic Skills for the TOEFL® iBT

Iain Donald Binns
Jonathan Wrigglesworth

Compass
Publishing

Listening 3

Basic Skills for the TOEFL® iBT 3

Listening

Iain Donald Binns · Jonathan Wrigglesworth

© 2008 Compass Publishing

Project Editor: Liana Robinson
Acquisitions Editor: Emily Page
Content Editor: Alexander Page
Copy Editor: Casey Malarcher
Contributing Writer: Micah Sedillos
Consultants: Lucy Han, Chanhee Park
Cover/Interior Design: Dammora Inc.

email: info@compasspub.com
http://www.compasspub.com

ISBN: 978-1-59966-159-9

10 9 8 7 6 5 4
12 11 10 09

Contents

Introduction to the TOEFL® iBT

What is the TOEFL® test?

The TOEFL® iBT test (Test of English as a Foreign Language Internet-based test) is designed to assess English proficiency in non-native speakers who want to achieve academic success as well as effective communication. It is not meant to test academic knowledge or computer ability; therefore, questions are always based on material found in the test.

The TOEFL® iBT test is divided into four sections:

- Reading
- Listening
- Speaking
- Writing

TOEFL® Scores

TOEFL® scores can be used for:

- Admission into university or college where instruction is in English
- Employers or government agencies who need to determine a person's English ability
- English-learning institutes who need to place students in the appropriate level of English instruction

It is estimated that about 4,400 universities and other institutions require a certain TOEFL® test score for admission.

The exact calculation of a TOEFL® test score is complicated and not necessary for the student to understand. However, it is helpful to know that:

- Each section in the Internet-based test is worth 30 points
- The highest possible score on the iBT is 120 points
- Each institution will have its own specific score requirements

✻ It is very important to check with each institution individually to find out what its admission requirements are.

Registering for the TOEFL® iBT

Students who wish to take the TOEFL® test must get registration information. Registration information can be obtained online at the ETS website. The Internet address is www.ets.org/toefl.

The website provides information such as:

- testing locations
- identification requirements
- registration information
- costs
- other test preparation material
- test center locations

This information will vary depending on the country in which you take the test. Be sure to follow the requirements carefully. If you do not have the proper requirements in order, you may not be able to take the test. Remember that if you register online, you will need to have your credit card information ready.

Introduction to the Listening Section of the TOEFL® iBT

In the listening section of the TOEFL® test, you will hear a variety of conversations and lectures, each of which lasts from 3–6 minutes. A total of six listening passages will be presented. After each passage, you will then be asked to answer 5–6 questions about what you heard. These questions are designed to test your ability to

- recognize and understand the main idea
- determine factual information
- determine inference

You will not be asked questions regarding vocabulary or sentence structure. You will not be permitted to see the questions until after you have listened to the conversation or lecture. Although some questions will replay part of the conversation or lecture, you cannot choose to listen to it again while answering the questions. You do not need any previous knowledge on the topic in order to answer the questions correctly.

Passage Types

1. Conversations—two people discussing a campus-related problem, issue, or process
2. Lectures—a professor speaking a monolog, presenting information related to an academic topic
3. Classroom interaction—similar to the lecture passage type, but with some interaction between the professor and one or more students

Listening Question Types

Most questions will be normal multiple-choice. However, the other types are

- multiple-choice questions with more than one answer
- replay questions where the test taker will listen to part of the conversation again before choosing the correct answer
- questions that asks the test taker to put events or steps of a process in order
- questions that require the test taker to match text or objects to a category

The following list explains the types and number of each question per listening passage on the TOEFL® iBT test. Questions may not always appear in this order.

Question Type	Number	Description
Main Idea	1	Choose the best phrase or sentence
Detail	1–2	Choose the statement that is true according to the listening passage
Function	1–2	Choose the answer that explains why the speaker has said something
Attitude	1–2	Choose the answer that describes the speaker's emotion, attitude, or opinion
Organization	0–1	Explain how or why the speaker communicated certain information
Content	0–1	Select the answers that feature points from the listening passage

Most questions are worth 1 point each; however, some may be worth more.

Test management:

- A visual image will be given on the screen to allow test takers to recognize each speaker's role and the context of the conversation.
- Before you begin the listening section, listen to the headset directions. Pay particular attention to how you change the volume. It is very important that you be able to hear clearly during the listening section of the test.
- If you miss something that is said in a conversation or lecture, do not panic. Forget about it and simply keep listening. Even native speakers do not hear everything that is said.
- Note-taking during the lecture is permitted. Paper will be provided by the test supervisor. These notes can be studied while answering the questions.
- Like the reading section, questions cannot be viewed until after the lecture/conversation has been completed.
- You must answer each question as it appears. You can NOT return to any questions later.
- Do not leave any questions unanswered. You are NOT penalized for guessing an answer.

[01] Conversation

Getting Ready to Listen

A. Learn the words.

Key Vocabulary

bridge	something that provides a link or connection between two things
public relations	the profession of promoting a positive image of a company or person to the public
marketing	the profession of presenting products in such a way as to make them desirable
industry	the different companies connected with the making and selling of a particular product or range of products
work experience	experience you have gained in a certain field

TOEFL® Vocabulary

consult	to ask a specialist for advice or a professional for information
incorporate	to combine one thing with another so as to form a united whole
attend	to go to, or be present at, an event
ongoing	continuing now and for some time to come
criteria	the standard for judging things by

B. Learn the question type.

TOEFL® Question Type

Main Idea

What problem does the man/woman have?

Why is the man/woman talking to the professor/librarian/etc.?

Why does the professor ask to see the student?

• Incorrect answer choices might include minor details from the conversation.

• The correct answer choice will summarize why the speakers are talking.

Practice

A. **Listen to the first part of the conversation and choose the correct answers.**
Track 1-1

1. What is the main topic of this conversation?

   (A) The student wants to complain about the degree she is studying.

   (B) The student wants to find out more about another degree program.

2. How does the professor explain what the communication degree is?

   (A) He tells her what she must do to enter it and then lists the subjects involved.

   (B) He gives her a book explaining what the degree is about.

Note-taking

B. **Listen to the full conversation and take notes.** Track 1-2

Woman - Student	Man - Professor
• Decided to _____ _____	• Will have to _____ _____
• Asking about _____ _____	• Course looks at _____ _____
• Doesn't enjoy _____ _____ _____ _____ _____ _____ _____	• Will also study _____ _____ _____ _____ _____ _____ _____

C. Choose the correct answers.

1. What problem does the woman have?

(A) She is not enjoying her degree and would like to change it to another.

(B) She does not like the university and would like to leave.

2. What is the main topic of the conversation?

(A) A description of what is involved in studying the Communication Degree

(B) A discussion of the things that the student must do in order to change degrees

3. Why does the professor say this: ( )?   Track 1-3

(A) To find out what the student's attitude toward the degree is

(B) To emphasize that work experience only makes up a small part of the degree

TOEFL® Vocabulary Practice

D. Fill in the blanks with the correct words.

consult	incorporate	attend	ongoing	criteria

1. Members of your family normally _____ your wedding.

2. If the crime has not been solved, the investigation would be _____.

3. Students should stick to the _____ of an exam to get the best marks.

4. When people are very ill, they will _____ a doctor for advice.

5. All cars _____ many different moving parts.

Test

Listen to the conversation and take notes. **Track 1-4**

Man - Student	Woman - Professor
• Considering _____ _____	• Has a _____ _____
• Wants to know _____ _____ _____	• Class made up of _____ _____ _____

Choose the correct answers. **Track 1-5**

1. Why is the man speaking to the professor?

(A) He would like to sign up for a graphic design class.

(B) He wants to find out what is involved in the marketing class.

(C) He would like to know how the graphic design class is graded.

(D) He would like the professor's advice on what class he should sign up for.

2. According to the professor, why is work experience not a part of the graphic design class?

(A) The class is not long enough for students to get work experience.

(B) The class is focused on written work and not practical experience.

(C) Students must attend all classes and so could not leave to get work experience.

(D) Students will not learn the skills needed to work properly in the industry.

3. What is the student's opinion of the assessments that occur in the graphic design class?

(A) He is frustrated by the ongoing assessments.

(B) He is anxious about the attendance requirements.

(C) He is happy with the lack of large exams at the end of the class.

(D) He is worried that there are too many assessments throughout the class.

4. In the conversation, the professor mentions the different ways in which students are assessed in the graphic design class. Indicate whether each of the following is mentioned. For each phrase, check the YES or NO column.

	YES	NO
(A) Written work marked throughout the class		
(B) Final exams at the end of the class		
(C) Individual projects throughout the year		
(D) Ongoing Work Experience		

Lecture - History

Getting Ready to Listen

A. Learn the words.

industrial	relating to industry or the people working in it
textile	cloth or goods produced by weaving
workshop	a room or small building used for making and repairing things
fortune	a large amount of money
raw material	natural unprocessed material

TOEFL® Vocabulary

revolution	a complete change in ways of thinking and methods of working
migration	when many people or animals move to another place
workforce	the people who work in a particular industry, company, or country
restrict	to limit or control something or someone
export	to sell goods to another country

B. Learn the question type.

TOEFL® Question Type

Main Idea

What aspect of X does the professor mainly discuss?

What is the main topic of the talk?

• Incorrect answer choices might include minor details from the lecture.

• The correct answer choice will summarize what the whole lecture is about or why it is being given.

Practice

A. Listen to the first part of the lecture and choose the correct answers. `Track 1-6`

1. What is the main topic of this lecture?

(A) The conditions that led to the Industrial Revolution (B) Migration

2. What are the key points of this lecture?

(A) Migration, the textile industry, and Europe

(B) The rule of law, an increased workforce, and improved railroads and shipping

3. How does the professor describe the main topic?

(A) By giving problems and solutions

(B) By defining concepts

4. Choose the best note-taking diagram for this lecture.

(A) Venn Diagram　　　　(B) Problem and　　　　(C) Concept Defining
　　　　　　　　　　　　　　　Solution Diagram　　　　　Diagram

Note-taking

B. Draw the diagram chosen in question 4. Then insert the information from questions 1 and 2.

C. Now listen to the full lecture and complete your notes. `Track 1-7`

D. Choose the correct answers.

1. What is the lecture mainly about?

    (A) How and why the Industrial Revolution began

    (B) Where the Industrial Revolution took place

2. What aspect of the workforce does the professor mainly discuss?

    (A) Availability   (B) Health

3. What can be inferred from the introduction of the rule of law?

    (A) Most people would have thought it was a good idea.

    (B) Most people would have thought it was a bad idea.

TOEFL® Vocabulary Practice

E. Fill in the blanks with the correct words.

revolution	migration	restrict	workforce	exports

1. In most countries, there are laws that _____ people from owning a gun.

2. Many tribes follow the _____ of animal herds.

3. Some people think we are in the middle of a technology _____.

4. Australia _____ beef to Asia.

5. In today's economy, it's important for businesses to have an educated

    _____.

Test

🎧 Listen to the lecture and take notes. `Track 1-8`

> ## Industrial Revolution: Social Changes
>
> - Factories
>
> - Cities
>
> - Families

- First factories

- Migration to cities

- Working outside of home

Choose the correct answers. `Track 1-9`

1. What is the main idea of the lecture?

    (A) Because of the Industrial Revolution, a lot of cities were built.

    (B) During the Industrial Revolution, many factories were built.

    (C) There were a lot of social changes as a result of the Industrial Revolution.

    (D) During the Industrial Revolution, people used coal to decorate their houses.

2. According to the professor, why were factories built near transportation centers?

   (A) So that it would be possible for people to get buses and trains to work

   (B) So that it would be possible to move raw materials to the factories and export goods overseas

   (C) Because there was an existing workforce in the cities

   (D) Because the majority of the workforce lived in cities

3. What is the purpose of the student's response?

   (A) To inform the professor that people were affected by the Industrial Revolution

   (B) To inform the professor of a social change

   (C) To show the professor that she understands what he said

   (D) To tell the professor that people at this time underwent a big change

4. What is the professor's attitude toward child labor?

   (A) He encourages it.

   (B) He is pleased it is outlawed.

   (C) He thinks it is acceptable in some situations.

   (D) He doesn't give his opinion.

5. How did the professor organize the information about the social effects of the Industrial Revolution?

   (A) By giving the problems then the solutions

   (B) By showing causes and effects

   (C) By giving specific examples of change

   (D) Chronologically

6. In the lecture, the professor described social changes that resulted from the Industrial Revolution. Indicate whether each of the following is mentioned.

	YES	NO
(A) Cities		
(B) Workforce		
(C) Food		
(D) Schools		
(E) Families		

Check-up

A. Choose the correct answers.

1. When answering a conversation main idea question

   (A) choose the answer choice that states the reason why the speakers are talking
   (B) choose the answer choice with minor details from the conversation
   (C) choose the answer that explains why a speaker asks a certain question
   (D) choose the answer that puts the steps of a sequence into the correct order

2. What should you do when answering a lecture main idea question?

   (A) Select the answer that includes a minor detail from the lecture.
   (B) Select the answer choice that best explains the speaker's opinion.
   (C) Select the answer that best contradicts the main idea of the lecture.
   (D) Select the answer choice that summarizes what the whole lecture is about.

Key Vocabulary Practice

B. Fill in the blanks with the correct words.

industrial	textiles	workshop	fortune	raw material
bridge	public relations	marketing	industry	work experience

1. Coal is a type of _____.

2. As oil supplies are getting lower, the oil _____ has to raise its prices.

3. Some people spend a(n) _____ when they go shopping.

4. In order to get a good job, it is helpful to have some _____.

5. My father has a(n) _____ where he likes to fix things.

6. London _____ connects the two sides of the Thames river.

7. Most cities have a(n) _____ area where there are a lot of factories.

8. _____ companies often look at packaging to make a product look nicer.

9. Today, many of the _____ used to make clothing are not natural.

10. Celebrities often work with _____ companies to improve their public images.

[02] Conversation

Getting Ready to Listen

A. Learn the words.

as a matter of fact	actually
student card	an identification card with a student's information on it
establish	to confirm the truth of something
desirable	worthy of having or doing
deposit	money given as a security against possible damage or loss

TOEFL® Vocabulary

locate	to discover where something is
input	to enter data into a computer
somewhat	to some extent or degree
initial	present at the beginning of an event or process
administrate	to oversee or organize the affairs of something

B. Learn the question type.

TOEFL® Question Type

Detail

What happened to X?

What does the man want to know?

In this conversation, what does X mean?

- Incorrect answer choices may repeat the speakers' words but convey a different meaning than the question asks.
- Incorrect answer choices may include information not mentioned by the speakers.

Practice

A. Listen to the first part of the conversation and choose the correct answers.
`Track 1-10`

1. What is the main topic of this conversation?

   (A) The student would like to change apartments in the student accommodation.

   (B) The student would like to extend his stay in student accommodation.

2. How does the student explain that he would like to extend his stay?

   (A) He asks the university worker to extend the lease on his apartment.

   (B) He explains that he would like to talk about extending his stay and asks if it is possible to do so.

Note-taking

B. Listen to the full conversation and take notes. `Track 1-11`

Man - Student	Woman - University Employee
• Would like to _____	• Students can extend but _____
• Staying in _____	• The apartments are _____
• Will go into _____	• Would not have to _____

C. Choose the correct answers.

1. What is the conversation mainly about?

(A) The student wants to arrange for his stay in student accommodation to be extended.

(B) The student wants to find out how much it would cost for another year in student accommodation.

2. According to the student, what is his reason for wanting to extend his stay?

(A) He has grown attached to his apartment over the last year and would like to keep it for his final year.

(B) He does not want to lose any of his deposit or spend money on another one.

3. What resulted from the conversation between the student and the university worker?

(A) He was unable to extend his contract for the full year, as too many students have requested the apartments.

(B) The university worker decided to extend his stay in the accommodation over the summer and the following school year.

TOEFL® Vocabulary Practice

D. Fill in the blanks with the correct words.

locate	input	somewhat	initial	administrate

1. In an office, it is often a secretary's job to _____ office affairs.

2. On a world map, you can _____ countries all over the world.

3. I didn't really like the movie; it was _____ boring.

4. Computer programmers have to _____ a lot of data into computers.

5. The president was present at the _____ meeting of the two countries.

Test

Listen to the conversation and take notes.   **Track 1-12**

Woman - Student	Man - University Employee
• Is an _____ _____	• Needs to see _____ _____
• Going to _____ _____	• It is easier _____ _____
• Wants to know _____ _____ _____ _____ _____	_____ _____ _____ _____ _____

Choose the correct answers.   **Track 1-13**

1. Why does the student go to speak to the university worker?

    (A) To find out if she will be able to study at the school the following semester
    (B) To ask whether or not she will be able to stay in student accommodation next semester
    (C) To explain that she would like to change apartments next semester
    (D) To inform the school that she will not need student accommodation next semester

2. According to the university worker, why is it easier for students to change apartments?

    (A) It is cheaper for students to pay for a new apartment.
    (B) There are a lot of forms to fill out when keeping the same apartment.
    (C) It can take a long time to organize deposits when keeping an apartment.
    (D) Many students like to change apartments at the end of a semester.

3. Why does the student say this: 🎧 ?

    (A) To inform the university worker that she does not like the student accommodation
    (B) To explain that she would be happy to keep her current apartment
    (C) To express her dislike for small apartments
    (D) To confirm that she would like to change apartments if possible

4. Why does the university worker talk about the difficulties of organizing deposits when keeping an apartment?

    (A) To encourage the student to change apartments as it will be easier to do
    (B) To explain that it could take the student some time to get her deposit back
    (C) To emphasize that he is very busy
    (D) To discourage the student from seeking further student accommodation

Lecture - Visual Arts

Getting Ready to Listen

A. Learn the words.

focus	sharpness of image
set	the scenery, furniture, etc. used on a stage in a play or in the place where a film is made
narrow	measuring only a small distance from one side to the other
choppy	rough; jerky; shifting
special effect	an unusual and artificial image or sound used in movies and TV shows

so-called	usually called
widespread	happening in many places or situations
vision	the area that you can see
interaction	the process of talking or working with other people
progression	a gradual change, from one state to another

Detail

How does the professor emphasize her point about X?

How does the professor define X?

Select the drawing/diagram that shows X?

- Incorrect answer choices may include information that is inaccurate or contradicts what the professor says.
- Incorrect answer choices may include similar-sounding words to those used by the professor, but do not include the same information.

Practice

A. **Listen to the first part of the lecture and choose the correct answers.** `Track 1-14`

1. What is the main topic of this lecture?

   (A) The differences between *Citizen Kane* and modern movies
   (B) The differences between movies made before *Citizen Kane* and after *Citizen Kane*

2. What are the key points of this lecture?

   (A) Photography, changes between scenes, and make-up
   (B) *Citizen Kane*, Orson Welles, and modern movies

3. How will the professor describe the main topic?

   (A) By comparing and contrasting   (B) By defining concepts

4. Choose the best note-taking diagram for this lecture.

   (A) Cause and Effect   (B) Concept Defining   (C) Venn Diagram
       Diagram   Diagram

`Note-taking`

B. **Draw the diagram chosen in question 4. Then insert the information from questions 1 and 2.**

C. **Now listen to the full lecture and complete your notes.** `Track 1-15`

D. Choose the correct answers.

1. In older movies, why was the interaction between actors unnatural?

(A) There was no sound.

(B) The actors couldn't move around much.

2. According to the professor, what is one way that deep focus photography affected movies?

(A) It allowed actors to move around the set.

(B) It introduced the techniques used in the special effects makeup.

3. What resulted from the way Orson Welles used sound in his movies?

(A) Smoother scene changes

(B) Choppier scene changes

TOEFL® Vocabulary Practice

E. Fill in the blanks with the correct words.

so-called	widespread	vision	interaction	progression

1. If someone has 20/20 _____, they can see well.

2. Most people didn't think the _____ best movie of the year was that good.

3. The movie's _____ was so slow that many people found it boring.

4. There is often little _____ between teachers and students outside of class time.

5. There was _____ panic on the Titanic after it hit the iceberg.

Test

🎧 Listen to the lecture and take notes. `Track 1-16`

Welles: Comparison of sound between *Citizen Kane* and *War of the Worlds*

- Changes between scenes

- Actors' voices

- Background crowd noise

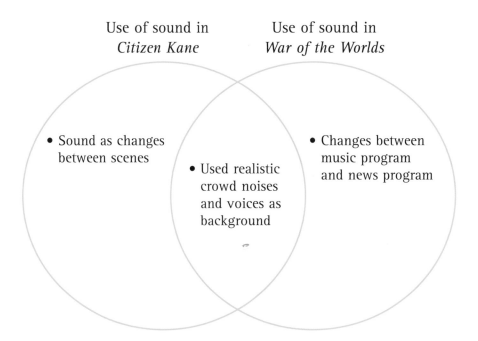

Use of sound in
Citizen Kane

Use of sound in
War of the Worlds

- Sound as changes between scenes

- Used realistic crowd noises and voices as background

- Changes between music program and news program

Choose the correct answers. `Track 1-17`

1. What is the main topic of the lecture?

(A) The progression of *Citizen Kane* and *War of the Worlds*

(B) How *Citizen Kane* and *War of the Worlds* were made

(C) How many listeners believed aliens were invading when they heard *War of the Worlds*

(D) How Orson Welles used sound to create realism in *Citizen Kane* and *War of the Worlds*

2. According to the professor, what happened when the radio program *War of the Worlds* aired?

(A) Listeners thought it was excellent.

(B) Listeners thought Orson Welles was taking over the world.

(C) Listeners thought it was a real news broadcast.

(D) Nobody listened to it.

3. What can be inferred from the professor's response?

(A) That she wouldn't know if the people were stupid, as she is not stupid

(B) That she doesn't know anything about stupid people

(C) That she doesn't think the people were stupid, just tricked

(D) That she thinks the student is stupid

4. What is the professor's opinion of *War of the Worlds*?

(A) She thinks it was very realistic.

(B) She thinks it was better than *Citizen Kane*.

(C) She didn't like it.

(D) She thinks it should be broadcast again.

5. Why does the professor mention that the actors in *War of the Worlds* made mistakes?

(A) Because she wants the students to know that the actors weren't very good

(B) Because the students asked her to

(C) To give an example of how widespread the panic was

(D) To give an example of one of the methods Welles used to make the broadcast seem real

6. What can be inferred about the *War of the Worlds* broadcast?

(A) It was very popular.

(B) It frightened many people.

(C) It made people laugh.

(D) Nobody listened to it.

Check-up

A. Choose the correct answers.

1. When answering a conversation detail question
    (A) pick the answer that best describes what the speaker's main problem is
    (B) choose the answer that repeats the speakers' words but conveys a different meaning
    (C) pick the answer that includes descriptions or examples mentioned by the speakers
    (D) choose the answer that includes information not mentioned by the speakers

2. What should you do when answering a lecture detail question?
    (A) Select the answer that contradicts information mentioned by the professor.
    (B) Select the answer that includes facts or definitions mentioned by the professor.
    (C) Select the answer that includes information that can be inferred from the professor's attitude.
    (D) Select the answer that explains why the professor tells a certain story during the lecture.

Key Vocabulary Practice

B. Fill in the blanks with the correct words.

focus	set	student card	choppy	special effects
as a matter of fact	narrow	establish	desirable	deposit

1. Every play needs a(n) _____ designer.
2. During a storm, the waves at sea are _____.
3. _____ roads were common before cars became popular.
4. Some people find it difficult to _____ on a lecture if it is a new subject for him or her.
5. Horror movies usually have a lot of _____.
6. When a student first goes to university, he or she will receive a(n) _____.
7. When a rented apartment is damaged, the repairs will come out of the occupant's _____.
8. _____, I left my ticket for the concert at home.
9. Members of the public often see the celebrity lifestyle to be _____.
10. It is the job of the police to _____ the truth about what happened when a crime is committed.

[03] Conversation

Getting Ready to Listen

A. Learn the words.

Key Vocabulary

prearrange	to arrange or plan beforehand
field	a subject or activity, often within a business or profession
junior	a student in the third year of university
anonymous	unknown; nameless
fill out	to supply information usually by form

TOEFL® Vocabulary

internship	a program that provides practical experience for beginners in an occupation or profession
convention	the gathering of people for a common interest
confirm	to verify; to validate
supervisor	a person who oversees and guides the work of other people
estimate	to make an approximation; to make a guess

B. Learn the question type.

TOEFL® Question Type

Function

Why does the student go to see the professor?

What does the student imply when he/she says this: 🎧 ?

Why does the student say this: 🎧 ?

You will hear part of the conversation again.

- Incorrect answer choices may suggest reasons not supported by the words spoken in the conversation.
- Incorrect answer choices may have reasons contradictory to the tone of the speaker's voice.

Practice

A. **Listen to the first part of the conversation, and choose the correct answers.**

Track 1-18

1. What is the main topic of the conversation?

    (A) A student who will interview for internships

    (B) How to prearrange interviews

2. How did the man organize his interviews?

    (A) By prearranging them and confirming them the day before

    (B) By calling the woman in the morning

Note-taking

B. **Listen to the full conversation and take notes.** Track 1-19

Male - Student	Woman - Employee
• Confirmed two _____ _____ _____ _____ _____ _____ _____ _____	• Asks if he has _____ _____ • There are quite a few _____ _____ • Quite a few _____ _____ • She estimates _____ _____ _____ _____

C. Choose the correct answers.

1. According to the woman, how many students get internships at the end of their junior year?

(A) Approximately 50%

(B) Approximately 85%

Listen again to part of the conversation and then answer the questions. Track 1-20

2. Why does the student say this: ?

(A) He confirmed his appointments but is not sure if the woman knows.

(B) The woman does not have his name down.

3. What can be inferred from the woman's response?

(A) He might not get his interview today because she can't find his name.

(B) She didn't mean to imply there was a problem; she just needed to check who he would see for his interview.

TOEFL® Vocabulary Practice

D. Fill in the blanks with the correct words.

internship	conventions	confirm	supervisor	estimate

1. To be a(n) _____, you have to be able to make a lot of decisions.

2. Job _____ usually display a number of different opportunities.

3. It is typical for students to get a(n) _____ before they graduate.

4. At the beginning of the semester, a professor will often _____ how many students in the class will pass it.

5. It is good to _____ doctor appointments before the appointment date.

Test

🎧 Listen to the conversation and take notes. [Track 1-21]

Woman - Student	Man - University Employee
• Is looking for the career office because _____ _____ _____ • Her major is _____ _____ • Had an internship _____ _____ _____ _____ _____	• Definitely can help • Can arrange a time to _____ _____ • 70% of _____ _____ _____ _____ _____ _____ _____ _____

Choose the correct answers. [Track 1-22]

1. What is the main topic of conversation?

(A) How great the architecture program is

(B) How to become a career counselor

(C) The process of setting up an appointment with a career counselor

(D) The career fair that is held every spring

2. What resulted from the student's initial question?

(A) An appointment with the career counselor

(B) A job

(C) An appointment the following week

(D) An internship

3. What does the student imply when she says this: 🎧 ?

(A) She would like to keep interning at the same company.

(B) She already has experience in the job field she would like.

(C) She likes the summertime.

(D) She hasn't had any work experience.

4. What does the employee mean when he says this: 🎧 ?

(A) The student has a great chance at getting a job.

(B) Every architect student gets a job right after they graduate.

(C) Only internships are available.

(D) There are few job openings and a lot of students applying.

Lecture - Life Sciences

Getting Ready to Listen

A. Learn the words.

Key Vocabulary

genome	a map of all of the genes in a cell of an organism
gene	a part of a cell in a living organism that controls how it looks and develops
chromosome	a rod-shaped structure that carries genes
bio-fuel	fuel made from something that was once living
toxin	poison

TOEFL® Vocabulary

manipulation	the control or influence of someone or something
highlight	to emphasize a point; to make something easy to notice or understand
dispose of	to get rid of something
detect	to notice or discover something
mechanism	a mechanical part of a machine; the assembled moving part(s) of a machine

B. Learn the question type.

TOEFL® Question Type

Function

What is the purpose of the professor's/student's response?

Why does the professor ask the class about X?

What does the professor imply when he/she says this: ⌒?

You will hear part of the lecture again.

- Incorrect answer choices may contain reasons not supported by the words spoken by the professor.
- Incorrect answer choices may contain explanations that cannot be inferred from the logical flow of the lecture.
- Incorrect answer choices may contain explanations that cannot be inferred from the professor's tone of voice.

Practice

A. **Listen to the first part of the lecture and choose the correct answers.** `Track 1-23`

1. What is the main topic of this lecture?
   (A) Genome science
   (B) Genes

2. What are the key points of this lecture?
   (A) Genome research can be used to make fuels, clean up pollution, and warn of pollution.
   (B) Genome research can be used to make machines and medicine.

3. How does the professor describe the main topic?
   (A) By comparing and contrasting
   (B) By giving problems and solutions

4. Choose the best note-taking diagram for this lecture.
   (A) Ordering Diagram
   (B) Problem and Solution Diagram
   (C) Cause and Effect Diagram

Note-taking

B. **Draw the diagram chosen in question 4. Then insert the information from questions 1 and 2.**

C. **Now listen to the full lecture and complete your notes.** `Track 1-24`

D. Choose the correct answers.

1. Why does the professor say this: ⌔ ? `Track 1-25`

(A) To make the student feel good about her answer

(B) To make the student feel bad about her answer

2. What does the professor mean when he says this: ⌔ ? `Track 1-26`

(A) Pollution is a problem that needs to be addressed now.

(B) Pollution is a problem we are going to have to address one day.

3. According to the professor, which of the following is true?

(A) Bio-fuels made from bacteria already exist.

(B) The world is running out of energy.

TOEFL® Vocabulary Practice

E. Fill in the blanks with the correct words.

manipulation	highlight	dispose	detected	mechanism

1. People often _____ key words in their textbooks.

2. You should _____ of your trash thoughtfully.

3. Some criminals use _____ to steal money.

4. It is crucial that the brake _____ of a car works properly.

5. Most modern buildings are fitted with a sensor that goes off when smoke is _____.

Test

Listen to the lecture and take notes. Track 1-27

Genome DNA Research

- Body

- Bacteria

- Virus

Problem	Solution
DNA in the body can cause disease	Run tests to see if a person has the DNA then turn off bit of DNA that causes disease

Choose the correct answers. Track 1-28

1. What is the lecture mainly about?

(A) Cancer
(B) Genetic diseases
(C) Manipulation
(D) The potential of DNA research to cure diseases

2. According to the professor, how can DNA research help cure diseases?

(A) By turning off DNA causing diseases in the body
(B) By turning off DNA causing diseases in bacteria
(C) By turning off DNA causing diseases in viruses
(D) All of the above

3. Why does the professor say this: 🎧 ?

(A) Because it has the potential to make a lot of money

(B) Because it has the potential to cure diseases

(C) Because it is a new field of research

(D) Because it allows you to manipulate bits of DNA

4. What is the professor's attitude toward DNA research?

(A) He's optimistic.

(B) He's negative.

(C) He's cautious.

(D) He's bored.

5. Why does the professor mention cancer?

(A) Because cancer has been cured by DNA research

(B) As an example of a disease caused by the body's DNA

(C) As an example of a disease caused by bacteria

(D) As an example of a disease caused by viruses

6. What is the likely outcome of turning off a bit of DNA that causes a disease?

(A) The disease will come back years later.

(B) The person may have problems because part of their DNA doesn't work.

(C) The person will be cured.

(D) There will be no change.

Check-up

A. Choose the correct answers.

1. When answering a conversation function question
   (A) choose the answer that includes important details from the lecture
   (B) pick the answer that best summarizes the main idea
   (C) choose the answer that best explains the speaker's opinion
   (D) pick the answer that best explains the speaker's tone of voice

2. What should you do when answering a lecture function question?
   (A) Select the answer that includes the most minor details from the lecture.
   (B) Pick the answer that details the pattern to which the points of the lecture are presented.
   (C) Select the answer that best explains the pattern to how the points in the lecture were presented.
   (D) Pick the answer that best explains how the repeated word fits into the logical flow of the lecture.

Key Vocabulary Practice

B. Fill in the blanks with the correct words.

genes	anonymous	bio-fuels	genome	toxins
prearrange	field	junior	fill out	chromosomes

1. When someone is good looking, people usually say they have good _____.

2. If there are _____ in a lake, all life in the lake might die.

3. If we know the _____ of an organism, we can know what it will look like.

4. We need sustainable _____ as we are running out of energy options.

5. _____ contain genes and are usually found in pairs.

6. Employers have their new employees _____ a form with their personal information so they can receive a paycheck.

7. In your _____ year of university, you should try to get an internship in the field you are interested in.

8. Mathematics is a hard _____ of study for a lot of people.

9. Many people like to remain _____ when they complete surveys.

10. It is less expensive to _____ air travel.

[04] Conversation

Getting Ready to Listen

A. Learn the words.

Key Vocabulary

tip	a word of advice
intimidating	discouraging through fear
especially	particularly
prepared	ready in advance; put together in advance
gather	to collect; to compile

TOEFL® Vocabulary

survey	a questionnaire (n); to ask questions (v)
participant	a person who takes part in an event or activity
consent	permission; agreement
intense	involving great effort or much activity
comprehension	the ability to understand the meaning of something

B. Learn the question type.

TOEFL® Question Type

Attitude

What is the man's/woman's attitude toward X?

What can be inferred from the man's/woman's response?

- Incorrect answers may provide inferences unrelated to the conversation.
- Incorrect answers may suggest attitudes based on the literal words spoken rather than on the tone of voice.

Practice

A. Listen to the first part of the conversation and choose the correct answers.
Track 1-29

1. What is the main topic of the conversation?
   (A) The student needs tips on how to interview people for a class project.
   (B) The student needs advice on how to gather information for her research project.

2. How does the student explain her problem?
   (A) She explains her problems and then asks the professor to help her write questions.
   (B) She explains her problem and then asks for help.

Note-taking

B. Listen to the full conversation and take notes. Track 1-30

Woman - Student	Man - Professor
• Needs advice on _____ _____	• It can be _____ _____
• This is her _____ _____ _____ _____ _____ _____ _____ _____	• The tips he gives her are: - Have a good _____ - Make sure people _____ _____ _____ _____ _____ _____

C. Choose the correct answers.

1. What is the professor's attitude toward the student?

(A) He is unwilling to help her.

(B) He is happy to help her.

2. What does the professor mean when he says this: 🎧 ? `Track 1-31`

(A) Be interested in what you are doing

(B) Make sure to get consent from people filling out surveys

3. What can be inferred from the woman's response? 🎧 `Track 1-32`

(A) The project is going to be easier than she thought.

(B) The project is going to be harder than she thought.

TOEFL® Vocabulary Practice

D. Fill in the blanks with the correct words.

survey	participate	consent	intense	comprehension

1. The electric company sent a(n) _____ to all of their customers to learn how to better serve them.

2. The school needed parental _____ for all students going on the class trip.

3. If you wanted to _____ in the school play, you would have to audition.

4. The final exam will show the _____ level of all the students.

5. Many people are afraid to hike Mount Everest because it is so _____.

Test

Listen to the conversation and take notes. `Track 1-33`

Woman - Student	Man - Professor
• Not looking forward to doing _____ _____	• The more you practice, _____ _____ _____
• It is intimidating to _____ _____ _____	• Should have good comprehension _____ _____
• Asks if there are any other _____ _____ _____ _____ _____	_____ _____ _____ _____ _____

Choose the correct answers. `Track 1-34`

1. What is the main topic of the conversation?

   (A) The date the final project is due
   (B) Interviewing people for the final project
   (C) Class grades
   (D) Test review

2. What does the professor say she should do for a good interview?

   (A) Practice
   (B) Have a good attitude
   (C) Have good comprehension of material
   (D) All of the above

3. What is the student's attitude toward having to do interviews?

   (A) Happy and excited
   (B) Annoyed
   (C) Shy and nervous
   (D) She doesn't care.

4. Why did the professor give the student tips on how to interview?

   (A) To help her feel more confident
   (B) So that she could do his interview later
   (C) Because she failed her last project
   (D) Because he doesn't trust her

Lecture - Human Biology

Getting Ready to Listen

A. Learn the words.

Key Vocabulary

muscle	the flesh inside your body that you use to move; flesh that connects your bones together
skeletal	relating to the bones inside a living thing; relating to a skeleton
striped	having lines or bands of color
twitch	a small, sudden movement
smooth	having no rough parts

TOEFL® Vocabulary

imply	to suggest something without saying it directly
interval	the period of time between two events
nevertheless	however; nonetheless; but
alternating	placed one after the other in a regular pattern
internal	inside your body

B. Learn the question type.

TOEFL® Question Type

Attitude

What is the professor's point of view concerning X?

What does the professor mean when he/she says this: ( )?

- Incorrect answers may provide inferences unrelated to the lecture.
- Incorrect answers may suggest attitudes based on the literal words spoken rather than on the tone of voice.

Practice

A. Listen to the first part of the lecture and choose the correct answers. `Track 1-35`

1. What is the main topic of this lecture?

   (A) How we use muscles   (B) The three types of muscles

2. What are the key points of this lecture?

   (A) Skeletal, heart, and smooth muscles
   (B) Motion and tension

3. How will the professor describe the main topic?

   (A) By discussing each category in turn
   (B) By presenting problems and their solutions

4. Choose the best note-taking diagram for this lecture.

   (A) Problem and   (B) Categorizing Diagram   (C) Venn Diagram
       Solution Diagram

Note-taking

B. Draw the diagram chosen in question 4. Then insert the information from questions 1 and 2.

C. Now listen to the full lecture and complete your notes. `Track 1-36`

D. Choose the correct answers.

1. What does the professor mean when she says this: ◯ ? `Track 1-37`

    (A) That skeletal muscle is the only type of muscle people know about

    (B) That skeletal muscle is the most well-known type of muscles

2. What is the professor's attitude toward cardiac muscles?

    (A) She thinks they are the most important type of muscle.

    (B) She thinks they are less important than other muscles because they are only found in the heart.

3. What does the professor mean when she says this: ◯ ? `Track 1-38`

    (A) Smooth muscles have stripes similar to skeletal and heart muscles.

    (B) Smooth muscles don't have stripes like skeletal and heart muscles.

TOEFL® Vocabulary Practice

E. Fill in the blanks with the correct words.

implies	interval	nevertheless	alternating	internal

1. As its name _____, *One Tree Hill* only has one tree on it.

2. Lungs are an example of a(n) _____ organ.

3. There is usually a(n) _____ between the first and second acts of a play.

4. Zebras have _____ black and white stripes.

5. Winter is a very cold time of year. _____, it is also a very pretty time.

Listen to the lecture and take notes. **Track 1-39**

Types of Bones

- Long
- Short
- Flat
- Irregular
- Round

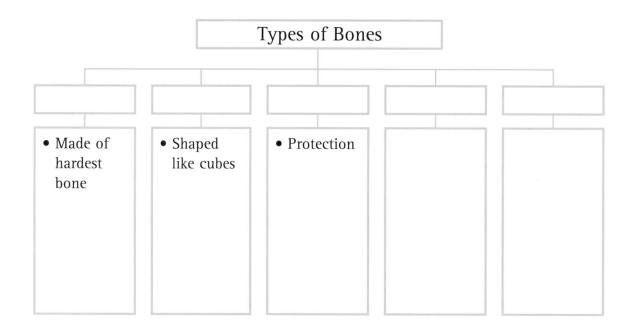

Types of Bones

• Made of hardest bone	• Shaped like cubes	• Protection		

Choose the correct answers. Track 1-40

1. What is the main topic of the lecture?

    (A) The classification of bones
    (B) The classification of muscles
    (C) The function of bones
    (D) The function of muscles

2. What are flat bones used for?

    (A) For grasping and holding
    (B) In joints
    (C) Movement
    (D) Protection

3. Why does the professor say this: 🔊 ?

    (A) To grab the students' attention
    (B) To introduce today's topic
    (C) To review the last lecture
    (D) To entertain the students

4. What can be inferred from the student's response: 🔊 ?

    (A) That he didn't attend the last lecture
    (B) That he understood the last lecture
    (C) That he wants to be a biology professor
    (D) That he isn't interested in science

5. Why does the professor mention knee caps?

    (A) As an example of a short bone
    (B) As an example of a flat bone
    (C) As an example of a long bone
    (D) As an example of a round bone

6. What can be inferred about round bones?

    (A) It would be difficult to move without them.
    (B) They are not needed.
    (C) They are the most well-known bones in the human body.
    (D) There are more of them than other types of bones in the human body.

Check-up

A. Choose the correct answers.

1. When answering a conversation attitude question
   (A) choose the answer that explains the main problem the students want solved
   (B) select the answer choice that provides an inference unrelated to the conversation
   (C) choose the answer that puts the steps of a sequence in the correct order
   (D) select the answer choice that includes an attitude best supported by the speaker's tone of voice

2. What should you do when answering a lecture attitude question?
   (A) Listen carefully for the main purpose of the lecture.
   (B) Listen carefully for clues in the professor's tone of voice.
   (C) Listen carefully for minor details about the main topic of the lecture.
   (D) Listen carefully for the correct sequence of steps in a process described by the professor.

Key Vocabulary Practice

B. Fill in the blanks with the correct words.

gather	skeletal	striped	intimidating	smooth
tips	twitch	especially	prepared	muscles

1. We use _____ muscles when we move.
2. At the beach, you can find stones that are worn _____ by sand.
3. A zebra looks like a(n) _____ horse.
4. An eye _____ is sometimes a sign that a person is nervous.
5. Weight lifters have big _____.
6. It is good to _____ information before you start a project.
7. The library is a good place to go study, _____ if you need to study where it is quiet.
8. If you want to get a good grade in a class, you should go to class _____ every day.
9. If you have never run in a race, your first time can be _____.
10. The professor gave the students _____ on how to do better on the exam.

[05] Conversation

Getting Ready to Listen

A. Learn the words.

Key Vocabulary

appointment	an arrangement to have a meeting
catering	the provision of food and drink for people at a function
disciplined	working in a controlled or systematic way
specialize	to devote time exclusively to an interest, skill, or field of study
placement	the act of an employment office filling a position

TOEFL® Vocabulary

graduate	to receive a degree or diploma from a school; to complete one's studies
afterward	at a later time or after an event that has been mentioned previously
passionate	having a keen enthusiasm or intense desire for something
face-to-face	in the physical presence of someone
categorize	to place someone or something in a particular category and define or judge the person or thing accordingly

B. Learn the question type.

TOEFL® Question Type

Organization

How does the man/woman organize information about X?

Why does the man/woman discuss X?

Why does the man/woman mention X?

- Organization questions are more commonly asked after lectures rather than conversations.
- Incorrect answer choices may suggest inaccurate connections between parts of the conversation.

Practice

A. Listen to the first part of the conversation and choose the correct answers.

Track 1-41

1. What is the main topic of this conversation?

   (A) The student wants to drop out of university to get a job.

   (B) The student needs some career advice for when he graduates.

2. How does the student explain his situation?

   (A) He explains that he will graduate soon but does not know what he should do next.

   (B) He asks for help to find a job and reveals that he has already graduated.

Note-taking

B. Listen to the full conversation and take notes. Track 1-42

Man - Student	Woman - University Worker
• Will graduate _____	• Assumes _____
• Looking for _____	• Will look for _____
• Would like to be _____	• Says it would be _____

C. Choose the correct answers.

1. Why does the student mention his specialization in making desserts and pastries?

(A) To explain that he loves making desserts

(B) To reinforce his strengths to potential employers

2. How does the student illustrate that he would be a good employee to hire?

(A) By listing a number of good qualities that he possesses

(B) By explaining that he has worked in kitchens before

3. What is the career counselor's attitude toward the student's skills?

(A) She is impressed by his qualities and believes he will easily find a job.

(B) She is worried that the student will not be a good employee.

TOEFL® Vocabulary Practice

D. Fill in the blanks with the correct words.

graduate	afterward	passionate	face-to-face	categorize

1. We talked to each other on the phone before we met _____.

2. Many students like to travel once they _____ from college.

3. We do not _____ milk as a vegetable because it comes from an animal.

4. I am _____ about model-making. I make them every day.

5. If you eat a big meal, it can be dangerous to go swimming _____.

Test

Listen to the conversation and take notes. **Track 1-43**

Woman - Student	Man - University Employee
• Looking for _____ _____	• Students should _____ _____
• Is a _____ _____ _____ _____ _____ _____	• Hard to _____ _____ _____ _____ _____ _____

Choose the correct answers. **Track 1-44**

1. Why is the student talking to the career counselor at the career office?

   (A) She would like some help finding a job once she graduates.
   (B) She is looking for advice on how to apply for jobs.
   (C) She is looking for some help in finding a summer work placement.
   (D) She is worried that she does not have much work experience and would like advice.

2. According to the student, which of the following is true?

   (A) She has never had a job before.
   (B) She is worried that she will not find a placement because she does not have much experience.
   (C) She is anxious that she does not have enough time to find a placement.
   (D) She feels that the career office will not be able to help her find work.

3. Why does the career counselor say this: ◠ ?

   (A) To imply that he does not think that the student will find a work placement
   (B) To apologize for not being able to find a work placement for the student
   (C) To reassure the student that she should still be able to find a placement
   (D) To emphasize that the student has no prior experience

4. How does the career counselor illustrate that experience is not vital to finding a work placement?

   (A) By mentioning that everybody has to start somewhere in their career
   (B) By stating that it is difficult to find work in biology
   (C) By defining "work experience"
   (D) By explaining that students can use the career office any time

Lecture - Business and Economics

Getting Ready to Listen

A. Learn the words.

Key Vocabulary

stock market	a particular market where stocks are traded
share	a part into which a company is divided
trade	to buy and sell goods or services
stock	a share in a company
broker	a person whose job is to buy and sell stocks for other people

TOEFL® Vocabulary

ignorant	lacking knowledge of something
historically	relating to the past
industrialized	having a lot of companies
depression	a period during which business, employment, and stock market values decline severely
chart	to record information over time, to see how it changes or develops

B. Learn the question type.

TOEFL® Question Type

Organization

How does the professor organize the information about X that he/she presents to the class?

How does the professor illustrate X?

Why does the professor discuss X?

- Incorrect answer choices may provide unconnected reasons for a specific action by the professor.
- Incorrect answer choices may suggest incorrect order to or connections between parts of the lecture.

Practice

A. Listen to the first part of the lecture and choose the correct answers. `Track 1-45`

1. What is the main topic of this conversation?

   (A) How to trade stocks successfully   (B) How to buy stocks successfully

2. What are the key points of this lecture?

   (A) Ignorant people, buying stocks, and making money
   (B) Decide on your goals, assess the market, and find a stock broker

3. How does the professor describe the main topic?

   (A) By giving the order in which to trade stocks
   (B) By giving examples of what stocks to trade

4. Choose the best note-taking diagram for this lecture.

   (A) Concept Defining   (B) Cause and Effect   (C) Ordering Diagram
        Diagram   Diagram

Note-taking

B. Draw the diagram chosen in question 4. Then insert the information from questions 1 and 2.

C. Now listen to the full lecture and complete your notes. `Track 1-46`

D. Choose the correct answers.

1. How is the discussion organized?

(A) By comparing modern and historical stock markets

(B) In steps that you should take to successfully trade stocks

2. Why does the professor suggest students pretend to buy and sell stocks?

(A) So that they become comfortable with the stock market before they begin trading with real stocks

(B) Because he thinks students are too ignorant to trade with real stocks

3. What does the professor mean when she says this: 🎧 ? **Track 1-47**

(A) Students should watch and take notes on what is happening in the stock market.

(B) Students should trade stationery items, such as pencils, for practice.

TOEFL® Vocabulary Practice

E. Fill in the blanks with the correct words.

ignorant	historically	industrialized	depression	chart

1. The employment _____ caused many people to lose their jobs.

2. _____, Australians have had close ties with Britain, because they are a member of the Commonwealth.

3. Some people who travel to Korea are _____ of Korean culture.

4. A good way to see how your savings plan is working is to _____ your savings.

5. Japan and Korea are _____ countries, whereas as Cambodia is not.

Test

🎧 Listen to the lecture and take notes. `Track 1-48`

The Great Depression

1. Black Tuesday
2. Bank failures
3. Drop in buying
4. Economic policies
5. Drought

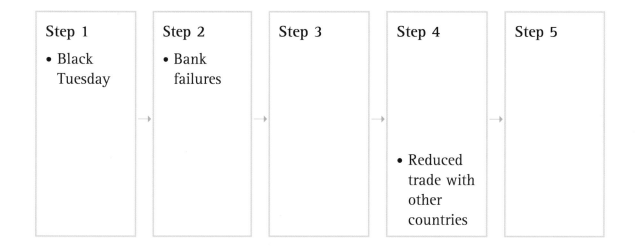

Step 1	Step 2	Step 3	Step 4	Step 5
• Black Tuesday	• Bank failures		• Reduced trade with other countries	

Choose the correct answers. `Track 1-49`

1. Why does the professor explain what an economic depression is?

(A) Because the topic of the lecture is depression

(B) Because the topic of the lecture is the Great Depression

(C) Because we are in an economic depression

(D) Because you need to know what an economic depression is to trade stocks

2. What is one way that a drop in buying can affect jobs?

(A) If no one buys things, companies stop making things, so there are fewer jobs.
(B) If no one buys things, stock prices go up.
(C) If no one buys things, severe drought can result.
(D) If no one buys things, banks will close.

3. Why does the professor say this: 🎧 ?

(A) So that the students will know how to buy the best stocks
(B) So that the students will know how to get rich from stocks
(C) So that the students will realize you can lose money in stocks
(D) So that the students will know the stock market always goes up

4. What can be inferred from the student's question: 🎧 ?

(A) The student is an economics major.
(B) The student wasn't listening.
(C) The student understands the stock market.
(D) The student doesn't understand the stock market.

5. How does the professor organize the discussion?

(A) She groups the ideas in categories.
(B) She presents problems and solutions.
(C) She compares and contrasts information.
(D) She presents the information in the order that it happened.

6. According to the lecture, which of the following happened during the Great Depression?

	Yes	No
(A) People lost money they had in the stock market.		
(B) People lost money they had in the bank.		
(C) People lost money they had in their house.		
(D) People lost houses and farms.		

Check-up

A. Choose the correct answers.

1. When answering a conversation organization question
   (A) pick the answer that best illustrates the problem the student wants solved
   (B) select the answer that best supports the speaker's tone of voice
   (C) pick the answer that best explains the connections between parts of the conversation
   (D) select the answer that includes minor details from the conversation

2. What should you do when answering a lecture organization question?
   (A) Choose the answer that focuses on a minor detail from the lecture.
   (B) Choose the answer that best explains the professor's tone of voice.
   (C) Choose the answer that summarizes the main point of the lecture.
   (D) Choose the answer that best explains the strategy behind a specific action of the professor.

Key Vocabulary Practice

B. Fill in the blanks with the correct words.

stock market	placement	trade	appointment	broker
stocks	catering	disciplined	specialize	share

1. If you're serious about getting into the stock market, you will need to get a(n) _____.

2. Being a majority _____ holder means you own a large percentage of a company.

3. The safest kind of _____ to buy are blue chip or low risk.

4. The _____ can be risky; you might make a lot of money and you might lose a lot of money.

5. When you _____, you buy or sell stocks.

6. To serve food at weddings, _____ companies are often hired.

7. My brother was a lawyer that used to _____ in divorce cases.

8. Before getting a job, many students must complete an unpaid work _____.

9. I am trying to eat more healthily, but I find it hard to be _____.

10. When most people go to see the doctor, they make a(n) _____ first.

[06] Conversation

Getting Ready to Listen

A. Learn the words.

Key Vocabulary

junk food	unhealthy, often fatty food that does not form part of a healthy diet
obesity	the state of being heavily overweight
outdated	no longer in fashion or popular
nutrition	sources of nutrients that keep the body healthy
involuntary	exacted against someone's will or wishes

TOEFL® Vocabulary

rational	reasonable and sensible
advocate	to recommend or support something
behalf	as somebody's representative
discretion	the freedom or authority to make a decision about something
arbitrary	based on personal feelings or perceptions rather than on objective facts or reasons

B. Learn the question type.

TOEFL® Question Type

Content

What is the likely outcome of doing X then Y?

What does the man/woman imply about X?

Indicate whether each of the following was mentioned in the conversation.

- Questions asking for information to be organized into a table are more common after lectures.
- Incorrect answer choices may include inferences not supported by the speaker's words or attitude.
- Incorrect answer choices may include past actions or conditions instead of probable future actions or conditions.

Practice

A. Listen to the first part of the conversation and choose the correct answers.

Track 2-1

1. What is the main topic of this conversation?

(A) The student would like to know why the cafeteria menu plan has changed.

(B) The student would like to order pasta salad.

2. How does the university employee explain that the menu has changed?

(A) She explains the school board's decision and offers the student a substitute.

(B) She lists the reasons why junk food is bad for students.

Note-taking

B. Listen to the full conversation and take notes. Track 2-2

Man - Student	Woman - University Employee
• Would like to _____ _____	• School canteen _____ _____
• Wants to know _____ _____	• School board _____ _____
• Thinks it _____	• Thinks the _____
• Is an _____	

C. Choose the correct answers.

1. According to the university worker, why did the school board make the decision to change the menu?

   (A) They wanted to promote a vegetarian lifestyle.

   (B) They were concerned by the lack of nutrition in young adults' diets.

2. In the conversation, the student describes a number of aspects of his life in response to the school board being able to change his diet. Indicate whether the following is mentioned. For each phrase, check the YES or NO column.

	Yes	No
(A) He is an active and healthy student.		
(B) He has been eating at the canteen for two years.		
(C) He has a problem with obesity.		
(D) He does not get regular exercise.		

3. Why does the university employee offer the student pasta and quiche?

   (A) To encourage the student to try a dish from the new healthy menu

   (B) To emphasize the importance of eating healthy food

TOEFL® Vocabulary Practice

D. Fill in the blanks with the correct words.

rational	advocate	behalf	discretion	arbitrary

1. The workers could not _____ the closing of the factory.

2. The decision to hire a potential employee is often at the manager's _____.

3. My brother thanked the generous donor on my _____.

4. The decision to go to that Chinese restaurant in particular was _____.

5. If you get lost, it is important to be _____ and not panic.

Listen to the conversation and take notes. `Track 2-3`

Woman - Student	Man - University Employee
• Would like _____ _____	• Recommends _____ _____
• Friends _____ _____ _____ _____ _____	• Only available _____ _____ • Policy of cafeteria _____ _____ _____

Choose the correct answers. `Track 2-4`

1. What is the conversation mainly about?

(A) The student is explaining that she is on a diet.

(B) The student wants to know why she cannot order what she would like.

(C) The student would like a recommendation on what to have for her lunch.

(D) The student would like to know the vegetarian options on the menu.

2. According to the student, what is the main problem with the cafeteria policy on set meals?

(A) She feels there is not enough variety on the menu.

(B) She feels the cafeteria will sell out of each dish quickly.

(C) She feels the set meals are too expensive.

(D) She feels customers should be able to order anything they would like.

3. What is the university employee's attitude toward the cafeteria policy of set meals?

(A) He is frustrated by all the complaints that he gets from students about it.

(B) He feels sympathy for the students but understands the reasons for the policy too.

(C) He is hopeful that the policy toward the set meals will soon be changed.

(D) He is angry that the students do not understand why the policy is in place.

4. In the conversation, the university employee states a number of reasons why the policy of only serving set meals is in place. Indicate which of the following is mentioned. For each phrase, check the YES or NO column.

	Yes	No
(A) It is easier for the cafeteria to know what to order.		
(B) There are not enough staff members to serve many dishes.		
(C) It is easy to monitor what food is popular.		
(D) There are too many students to cater to.		

Lecture - Cultural Studies

Getting Ready to Listen

A. Learn the words.

Key Vocabulary

pop culture	popular culture; music, films, etc. that are popular in a particular society
imitation	the act of copying or imitating
street fashion	fashion invented and worn by young people, not by fashion designers
racial	relating to the relationship between different races of people
dishonest	not honest; deceiving

TOEFL® Vocabulary

dominant	more powerful, important, or noticeable than other people or things
ethnic	relating to groups of people sharing culture, religion, race, etc.
discrimination	the practice of treating a member or members of a group differently and unfairly
bias	an unfair preference for, or dislike of, something
encounter	to meet somebody or something, usually unexpectedly

B. Learn the question type.

TOEFL® Question Type

Content

In the lecture, the professor describes X. Indicate whether each of the following is mentioned. Based on information in the lecture, indicate whether each sentence below describes X, Y, or Z. What does the professor imply about X?

- Questions asking for information to be organized into a table are more common after lectures.
- Incorrect answer choices may contain words that sound similar to those mentioned in the lecture but were not mentioned.
- Incorrect answer choices may include connections between parts of the lecture that are not supported by the lecture.

Practice

A. Listen to the first part of the lecture and choose the correct answers. `Track 2-5`

1. What is the main topic in this lecture?

   (A) The effect US entertainment has on other countries
   (B) The effect US policies have on other countries

2. What are the key points in this lecture?

   (A) Export of US entertainment leads to imitation, racial understanding, exposure to poor quality, and negative opinions of Americans.
   (B) Pop culture, street fashion, Oprah Winfrey, and violent movies

3. How does the professor describe the main topic?

   (A) By providing examples
   (B) By showing the cause and effect of certain aspects of US culture

4. Choose the best note-taking diagram for this lecture.

   (A) Categorizing Diagram   (B) Concept Defining Diagram   (C) Cause and Effect Diagram

 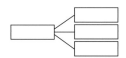

Note-taking

B. Draw the diagram chosen in question 4. Then insert the information from questions 1 and 2.

C. Now listen to the full lecture and complete your notes. `Track 2-6`

D. Choose the correct answers.

1. What is the likely outcome of people watching poor quality US TV shows?

   (A) They will be more understanding of ethnic diversity.

   (B) They will have a poor opinion of American entertainment.

2. What can be inferred from the passage?

   (A) TV shows that Americans watch are better than the US TV shows that are watched overseas.

   (B) All US TV shows are poor quality.

3. Why does the professor mention Oprah Winfrey?

   (A) To give an example of ethnic diversity in US entertainment

   (B) Because he thinks she is the best entertainer in the world

TOEFL® Vocabulary Practice

E. Fill in the blanks with the correct words.

pop culture	imitations	street fashion	racial	dishonest

1. You can create your own _____ by altering clothes that you already have.

2. Comedians often do good _____ of politicians.

3. _____ people often lie and steal.

4. Britney Spears is part of today's _____.

5. _____ discrimination remains a problem in many parts of the world.

Test

Listen to the lecture and take notes. **Track 2-7**

Breakdancing

- US → Korea

- Dance, contests

- Still alive

Breakdancing in US music videos	→	

	→	Dance, musicals, and contests in Korea

	→	

Choose the correct answers. **Track 2-8**

1. What effect of American culture does the professor mainly discuss?

(A) Negative opinions of American entertainment
(B) Negative opinions of Americans
(C) Racial diversity
(D) Imitation

2. What resulted from breakdancing being seen in US music videos overseas?

(A) It became popular in the US.
(B) It became popular in Korea.
(C) It became hated all over the world.
(D) Nothing changed.

3. What does the professor imply when she says this: 🎧 ?

    (A) That this is always the case

    (B) That Korea always does things better than America

    (C) That usually imitation isn't better

    (D) That it's normal for imitation to be better

4. What is the professor's opinion of Korean breakdancing?

    (A) It's the best in the world.

    (B) It's better than American breakdancing.

    (C) It's not very good.

    (D) Both A and B

5. How did the professor organize the information about the effect breakdancing has had on Korea?

    (A) By providing causes and effects

    (B) By giving examples

    (C) By defining concepts

    (D) By categorizing information

6. What does the professor imply about American breakdancing before it became popular in other countries?

    (A) It was the best in the world.

    (B) It wasn't very good.

    (C) It wasn't popular in America.

    (D) It was an imitation of Korean dance.

Check-up

A. Choose the correct answers.

1. When answering a conversation content question
    (A) choose the answer that includes an outcome that makes sense in connection with both the speaker's words and attitude
    (B) choose the answer that summarizes the problem the student wants to solve
    (C) select the answer that includes an action or situation that happened before the conversation
    (D) select the answer that best explains the speaker's emotions about the topic

2. What should you do when answering a lecture content question?
    (A) Choose the answers that include the information most often repeated in the lecture.
    (B) Pick the answers that correctly match the chart categories.
    (C) Choose the answers that include information least often mentioned in the lecture.
    (D) Pick the answers that cannot fit the categories given on the chart.

Key Vocabulary Practice

B. Fill in the blanks with the correct words.

nutrition	ethnic	discrimination	obesity	bias
junk food	encounter	outdated	involuntary	dominant

1. People _____ new cultures when they travel.
2. Gender _____ remains a problem in many organizations today.
3. Parents usually have a(n) _____ for their own children.
4. Brown eye genes are usually _____ over blue eye genes.
5. The US has a lot of _____ diversity, whereas Korea has very little.
6. Eating _____ every day can cause damage to your health.
7. Sally has a strict and old-fashioned father; she thinks his views are _____.
8. People who are concerned about _____ eat lots of fruit and vegetables.
9. When it is very cold and your teeth chatter, it is _____.
10. If someone is very overweight, they may suffer from _____.

[Review 1]

🎧 Listen to the conversation and take notes. **Track 2-9**

Woman - Professor	Man - Student
• Says student hasn't _____ • Asks if _____ • Is sorry to hear about _____ • Says last week, they _____ exam • Likes to _____	• Grandmother _____ so went home for _____ • Then, _____, so stayed home for _____

Choose the correct answers. **Track 2-10**

1. Why does the student visit the professor?

(A) Because he missed two weeks of classes, and he wants to let the professor know
(B) Because he is a conscientious student and often drops by the professor's office
(C) Because he missed two weeks of classes and wants to know if he missed a lot of work
(D) Because his grandmother died, and he wants to let his professor know

2. According to the professor, what is the main problem with the student missing the last two weeks of classes?

(A) He was not in class, so he was unable to give input for the mid-term exam.
(B) He is likely to fail the upcoming exam because he's not a good student.
(C) He has missed a lot, including the mid-term exam.
(D) He has missed a lot, including information about the mid-term exam.

3. What does the professor mean when she says this: 🎧 ?

(A) The student will have to study for about ten hours between now and the exam.
(B) The student is estimated to have about ten hours of exams ahead of him.
(C) There is about ten hours left before the exam.
(D) The student is going to have to study for the next ten hours.

4. What is the professor's attitude toward the student missing classes?

(A) She is empathetic and is sure the student will do well in the exam.
(B) She is empathetic, but she is also concerned about how the student will do in the exam.
(C) She is angry and isn't interested in helping the student.
(D) She is angry but says she will help the student anyway.

Listen to the lecture and take notes. **Track 2-11**

> ### Art movements of the early twentieth century
>
> • colors
>
> • bits of pictures
>
> • distorted reality

Fauvism

Cubism
• bits of the picture

Expressionism

Futurism
• wanted to rebel

Choose the correct answers. **Track 2-12**

1. What is the main topic of the lecture?

(A) The history of art in Europe

(B) Art movements of the early twentieth century

(C) The four most influential art movements in history

(D) Art movements of the early nineteenth century

2. According to the professor, what are Fauvist painters known for?

(A) Distorted reality
(B) Painting in bits
(C) Intense colors
(D) Patriotism

3. Why does the professor mention this: 🎧 ?

(A) To illustrate Fauvist painting style
(B) To show that the Fauvists were taught to think originally
(C) To show how much artists travel
(D) To illustrate the idea that artists must see the world before they begin to work

4. What is the professor's opinion of the colors used in Fauvist paintings?

(A) They distort reality.
(B) They are dull.
(C) They are beautiful.
(D) They show feelings.

5. Why does the professor mention WWI?

(A) It was an inspiration for many artists.
(B) It began around the time of the futurists.
(C) It brought an end to the Futurists.
(D) It stirred up feelings of patriotism in the Futurists.

6. Which of the following is true of Cubism? Place a checkmark in the correct box.

	True	False
(A) Picasso was a Cubist.		
(B) Cubists placed bits of their subject out of place.		
(C) Cubists were known for their intense colors.		
(D) Cubists were influenced by African art.		
(E) Cubist work was often patriotic and violent.		

Lecture 2

Listen to the lecture and take notes. Track 2-13

Hollywood and Bollywood

- Themes

- Length

- Actors

- variety of themes

- make movies

- dance and musicals

Choose the correct answers. Track 2-14

1. What is the lecture mainly about?

(A) That Bollywood makes the most movies

(B) A comparison of Hollywood and Bollywood movies

(C) Bollywood musicals

(D) The influence that Bollywood is having on Hollywood

2. According to the professor, what is the main theme of Bollywood movies?

(A) Action
(B) Romance
(C) Thriller
(D) Mystery

3. What does the professor mean when she says this: 🎧 ?

(A) Most people would be surprised by this fact.
(B) Most people know this fact.
(C) Most people agree with this statement.
(D) Most people don't know very much about movies.

4. What is the professor's attitude about the length of Bollywood movies?

(A) They are too long.
(B) They should be longer.
(C) They are fast paced, so they don't seem long.
(D) They become boring.

5. Why does the professor mention Bollywood movies being shown in the US and UK?

(A) To show that Bollywood movies are more popular than Hollywood movies
(B) To show that more Bollywood movies are shown worldwide than Hollywood movies
(C) To show that Bollywood movies are becoming more popular worldwide
(D) To illustrate the quality of Bollywood movies

6. Which of the following are true according to the lecture? Place a checkmark in the correct box.

	True	False
(A) Hollywood makes more movies than Bollywood.		
(B) Many Bollywood movies are romances.		
(C) The average Hollywood movie lasts two hours.		
(D) Some Bollywood actors work on ten movies at once.		
(E) Bollywood movies are only shown in India.		

Lecture 3

Listen to the lecture and take notes. **Track 2-15**

Protecting the Earth's Water Cycle

- Fresh water

- Waste

- Vegetation

Problem	Solution
→	
→	Protect vegetation and green space

Choose the correct answers. **Track 2-16**

1. What is the main topic of the lecture?

(A) Different forms of water: ice, liquid, and gas
(B) The disruption of the water cycle and what can be done
(C) How long water remains in glaciers
(D) How much fresh water there is in the world

2. According to the professor, what is one way clearing vegetation can affect the water cycle?

(A) Increase the amount of fresh water
(B) Increase evaporation
(C) Increase runoff
(D) Decrease rain

3. Why does the professor say this: ◯ ?

    (A) To introduce an illustrative example
    (B) To get the students' attention
    (C) To introduce a series of facts
    (D) To encourage the students' to think

4. What is the professor's attitude toward the shrinking supply of fresh water?

    (A) She is unconcerned.
    (B) She is concerned but believes it can't be stopped.
    (C) She is concerned and thinks there are actions we can take.
    (D) She thinks it isn't really shrinking.

5. Why does the professor mention that twenty-six countries are considered fresh water scarce?

    (A) To show that water shortages have always been a problem
    (B) To show that the supply of fresh water is a problem now
    (C) To explain what will happen as the supply of fresh water shrinks
    (D) To show how important the water cycle is

6. Which of the following is true according to the lecture? Place a checkmark in the correct box.

	True	False
(A) Only water in oceans goes through the water cycle.		
(B) Water can remain in a glacier for 65,000 years.		
(C) Water usually spends nine days in the water cycle.		
(D) The water cycle assures an unending supply of fresh water.		
(E) By 2025, it is estimated that we will have lost one-third of our fresh water.		

Listen to the conversation and take notes. Track 2-17

Woman - Student	Man - Librarian
• Looking for a _____	• Asks if the student _____
• Says she can't _____	_____
• Says doing well in assignment is	• Says they should _____
_____	• Agrees it's not there
• Says she _____	• Says the student can _____
_____	_____
_____	_____
_____	• Asks when _____
_____	_____
_____	_____
_____	_____

Choose the correct answers. Track 2-18

1. What problem does the woman have?

(A) She wants the man to order her a journal article to come on Monday.
(B) She wants the man to order her several books, and she needs them today.
(C) She needs to find a book in the library, but it's not on the right shelf.
(D) She needs to order a journal article for an assignment, but it might take a few days to come.

2. According to the man, what is the main problem with ordering the journal today?

(A) Unless they order it to come by express post, it won't arrive until Monday at the earliest.
(B) It will arrive on Monday but not before five o'clock.
(C) It will take up to a week to come and cost a lot of money.
(D) It won't arrive until Friday.

3. Why does the woman mention her plans to do an internship?

(A) To emphasize how important it is that she gets a good grade in the course she's doing
(B) Because she needs the librarian to help write her internship applications
(C) So that the librarian will help her get the journal article she needs before the internship begins
(D) Because her assignment is due next week, and her grades are lower than needed for the internship

4. What is the likely outcome if the woman orders the journal to come by express post?

(A) It will arrive during the weekend.
(B) It will arrive on Monday but not before five o'clock.
(C) It will arrive earlier, but will cost her money.
(D) It will arrive later, but will cost her money.

[07] Conversation

Getting Ready to Listen

A. Learn the words.

Key Vocabulary

in charge of	having the care or supervision of something
smoke detector	an electronic fire alarm that senses smoke and sounds an alarm in warning
master key	a key that will open a number of different locks
battery	a device that uses chemicals to produce an electric current, usually for small or portable devices
culprit	a person who is guilty of a crime or offense

TOEFL® Vocabulary

explicit	fully and clearly shown or expressed, leaving nothing to guess
forbid	to state that something must not be done
incredible	very surprising
genuine	honest and open in relationships with others
indiscretion	a lack of tact or good judgment

B. Learn the question type.

TOEFL® Question Type

Main Idea

What problem does the man/woman have?

Why is the man/woman talking to the professor/librarian/etc.?

Why does the professor ask to see the student?

• Incorrect answer choices might include minor details from the conversation.

• The correct answer choice will summarize why the speakers are talking.

Practice

A. Listen to the first part of the conversation and choose the correct answers.

Track 2-19

1. What is the main topic in this conversation?

   (A) The university employee is making a smoke alarm check in a student's room.

   (B) The university employee is changing smoke alarm batteries in students' rooms.

2. How does the university employee explain why he would like to go into the student's room?

   (A) By explaining who he is and that he is checking all of the student's rooms

   (B) By giving an example of what could happen if the student's smoke detector does not work

Note-taking

B. Listen to the full conversation and take notes.   Track 2-20

Woman - Student	Man - University Employee
• Removed _____ _____	• In charge of _____ _____
• Smokes _____ _____	• Has a _____ _____
• Doesn't like _____ _____ _____ _____ _____ _____ _____ _____	• Dorm policy _____ _____ _____ _____ _____ _____ _____

C. Choose the correct answers.

1. What are the speakers mainly discussing?

(A) The smoke alarm in the dorm room

(B) The batteries in the dorm room

2. Why does the university employee ask to see the student's dorm room?

(A) To check the smoke alarm

(B) To change the batteries in her smoke alarm

3. Why does the university worker say this: ◯ ? **Track 2-21**

(A) To explain to the student that she is lucky to be alive

(B) To emphasize that what the student has done was wrong

TOEFL® Vocabulary Practice

D. Fill in the blanks with the correct words.

indiscretion	explicit	forbid	incredible	genuine

1. When children misbehave, parents often _____ them from going out to play for a while.

2. She was _____ in her thanks for all of the gifts that she received.

3. The service at the hotel was so good it was _____.

4. My brother took full responsibility for his _____, so I accepted his apology.

5. The details in the instruction book for the stereo were _____.

Test

Listen to the conversation and take notes. **Track 2-22**

Woman - University Employee	Man - Student
• Had complaints _____ _____ • Student was _____ _____ _____ _____ _____ _____	• English _____ _____ • Forgot _____ _____ _____ _____ _____ _____

Choose the correct answers. **Track 2-23**

1. Why is the university worker speaking to the man?

(A) He asked to speak with her.

(B) He has been awarded something special.

(C) She believes that he did something bad.

(D) She wants to help him with a problem.

2. What was in the pot that the university worker found in the student's room?

(A) A rat

(B) Only water

(C) The man's breakfast

(D) The man's lunch

3. What can be inferred from the university worker's response: ◯?

(A) She understands the student's opinion more than the other students in the dorm.

(B) She does not believe the student's excuse.

(C) She thinks the student is confused.

(D) She believes that this is a very serious issue.

4. What will happen if the man is caught cooking in his room again?

(A) He will be evicted from the dormitories.

(B) He will be expelled from the school.

(C) He will be warned again.

(D) He will have to eat in the cafeteria.

Lecture - Literature

Getting Ready to Listen

A. Learn the words.

familiar	well known or easy to recognize
sonnet	a poem, usually of fourteen lines and often rhyming in a particular way
listing	a set of words or items, usually written one below the other
classify	to arrange by category or type
argument	a point or set of reasons used to try to convince someone of something

TOEFL® Vocabulary

appendix	a part of the end of a book containing additional information
contradiction	a difference between two statements, beliefs, or ideas that means they both cannot be true
aesthetic	how something looks; physical appearance
coherent	easy to understand because it is clear, connected, or linked together well
clarity	clearness; better or simpler understanding

B. Learn the question type.

TOEFL® Question Type

Main Idea

What aspect of X does the professor mainly discuss?

What is the main topic of the talk?

- Incorrect answer choices might include minor details from the lecture.
- The correct answer choice will summarize what the whole lecture is about or why it is being given.

Practice

A. Listen to the first part of the lecture and choose the correct answers. `Track 2-24`

1. What is the main topic in this lecture?

   (A) Shakespeare's plays   (B) Shakespeare's sonnets

2. What are the key points in this lecture?

   (A) Shakespeare had three categories of sonnets: The Fair Youth, The Dark Lady, and Others.

   (B) Shakespeare wrote over 150 sonnets and many were about a handsome young man.

3. How does the professor describe the main topic?

   (A) By giving examples

   (B) By comparing and contrasting

4. Choose the best note-taking diagram for this lecture.

   (A) Problem and   (B) Venn Diagram   (C) Concept Defining
   Solution Diagram   Diagram

Note-taking

B. Draw the diagram chosen in question 4. Then insert the information from questions 1 and 2.

C. Now listen to the full lecture and complete your notes. `Track 2-25`

80 | Listening |

D. Choose the correct answers.

1. What aspect of Shakespeare's work does the lecture mainly discuss?

   (A) Plays

   (B) Sonnets

   (C) Movies

   (D) Musicals

2. Why does the professor mention a good looking, handsome young man?

   (A) The man is a character related to some sonnets.

   (B) The professor is calling on a student in the class.

   (C) The man is Shakespeare.

   (D) The professor is remembering when he first read the sonnets.

3. What does the professor imply about Shakespeare's work?

   (A) That his sonnets are the least interesting of his work

   (B) That his movies are better than his plays and sonnets

   (C) That movies based on his plays are better than his plays

   (D) That his sonnets are less well known than his plays

TOEFL® Vocabulary Practice

E. Fill in the blanks with the correct words.

appendix	contradiction	aesthetics	coherent	clarity

1. It is important to relate ideas together so that your work is _____.

2. An interior designer is concerned with the _____ of the inside of a building.

3. Instructions are sometimes repeated for _____.

4. It would be a(n) _____ to say that soccer is your favorite sport and then argue that basketball is the best sport.

5. There is a useful list of verbs in the _____ of the book.

Test

Listen to the lecture and take notes. Track 2-26

Shakespeare's Plays

- Histories
- Comedies
- Tragedies

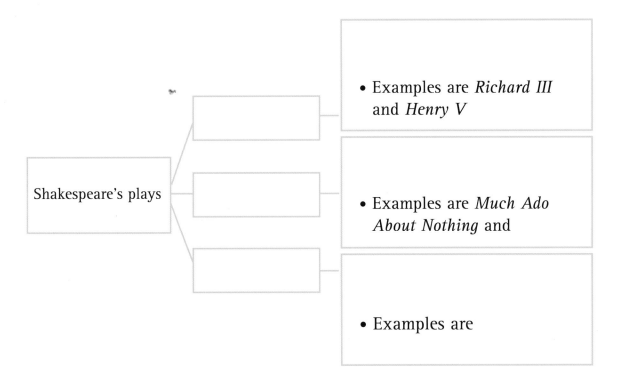

Shakespeare's plays

- Examples are *Richard III* and *Henry V*

- Examples are *Much Ado About Nothing* and

- Examples are

Choose the correct answers. Track 2-27

1. What is the main topic of the lecture?

(A) That the tragedies are Shakespeare's best plays

(B) The classification of Shakespeare's plays

(C) The poetry in Shakespeare's plays

(D) That the comedies are Shakespeare's best plays

2. According to the professor, what is true about the histories?

(A) They were too long.
(B) They were unclear.
(C) The poetry was simple.
(D) The stories were boring.

3. Why does the professor say this: 🎧 ?

(A) To show that Shakespeare wrote good plays
(B) To show that Shakespeare's tragedies are part of commonly known Western culture
(C) To show that *Romeo and Juliet* is the best of Shakespeare's tragedies
(D) To show that Shakespeare is still famous

4. What is the professor's opinion of Shakespeare's tragedies?

(A) They are full of simple poetry.
(B) They are too sad for modern audiences.
(C) They are Shakespeare's greatest plays.
(D) They took Shakespeare the longest time to write.

5. How is the discussion organized?

(A) By categories
(B) Cause and effect
(C) Chronologically
(D) Worst to best

6. What does the professor imply about *Romeo and Juliet*?

(A) It is Shakespeare's best play.
(B) It is one of Shakespeare's most famous play.
(C) It is the best play ever written.
(D) It is the best of Shakespeare's tragedies.

Check-up

A. Choose the correct answers.

1. When answering a conversation main idea question
   (A) choose the answer that best explains the problem the speaker wants solved
   (B) select the answer choice that focuses on a minor detail mentioned by one of the speakers
   (C) choose the answer that best explains the speakers' emotions about the topic
   (D) select the answer choice that demonstrates why the speaker asks a rhetorical question

2. What should you do when answering a lecture main idea question?
   (A) Select the answer that includes information that can be inferred from the professor's attitude.
   (B) Choose the answer that puts the steps of a sequence into the correct order.
   (C) Select the answer choice that best explains why the lecture is being given.
   (D) Choose the answer that best represents the pattern to which the points of the lecture are presented.

Key Vocabulary Practice

B. Fill in the blanks with the correct words.

familiar	sonnets	classified	listing	argument
smoke detector	master key	batteries	culprit	in charge of

1. Movie stars seem _____ because we have seen them in movies and on TV.

2. Most movies can be _____ as comedy, drama, thriller, horror, or romance.

3. Many people have written _____, but Shakespeare's are the most famous.

4. There are many good points in that _____, but I still disagree.

5. Dictionaries have a _____ of words and their definitions.

6. Most portable stereos need to have _____ in them to work.

7. The building security officer has a _____ for all of the rooms.

8. The _____ of the robbery was caught by the police in a hotel.

9. It is important to check often that the _____ in your home works.

10. A shop manager is _____ all of the other shop employees.

[08] Conversation

Getting Ready to Listen

A. Learn the words.

Key Vocabulary

merit	value that deserves respect and acknowledgment
article	a newspaper or reference piece
legacy	something that is handed down from a previous generation or time
strive	to try hard to achieve or get something
edition	one version of a publication issued serially or periodically

TOEFL® Vocabulary

unify	to bring people or things together to form a single unit or entity
liberal	tolerant of different views and standards of behavior in others
minority	a group of people, within a society, that have different characteristics from the rest of society
ambiguous	having more than one meaning
distortion	the describing or reporting of something in a way that is inaccurate or misleading

B. Learn the question type.

TOEFL® Question Type

Detail

What happened to X?
What does the man want to know?
In this conversation, what does X mean?

- Incorrect answer choices may repeat the speakers' words but convey a different meaning than the question asks.
- Incorrect answer choices may include information not mentioned by the speakers.

Practice

A. **Listen to the first part of the conversation and choose the correct answers.**
Track 2-28

1. What is the main topic in this conversation?

   (A) The student would like to buy a copy of the student newspaper.
   (B) The student is asking for a position at the student newspaper.

2. How does the student explain what she would like?

   (A) By explaining her motivation
   (B) By listing her qualifications

Note-taking

B. **Listen to the full conversation and take notes.**   Track 2-29

Woman - Student	Man - Newspaper Editor
• Would like to _____ _____	• Is _____ _____
• Is a _____ _____	• Says there are _____ _____
• Hopes to get _____	• Says the paper aims _____ _____
• Thinks the paper _____ _____	• Says the paper tries to _____ _____
• Is excited to _____ _____ _____ _____	• Says she must avoid _____ _____
	• Wants the _____ _____ _____

C. Choose the correct answers.

1. According to the student, why would she like a position at the newspaper?

(A) To build up some practical experience in journalism

(B) To meet other journalists while working there

2. Which of the following is true, according to the newspaper editor?

(A) There are very few available positions left at the newspaper.

(B) The paper tries to appeal to all groups and minorities in the school.

3. Why does the student go to see the newspaper editor?

(A) To question an article that was written in the newspaper

(B) To apply for a position at the newspaper

TOEFL® Vocabulary Practice

D. Fill in the blanks with the correct words.

liberal	unify	minority	ambiguous	distortion

1. In large cities, people from the same _____ often live close to one another.

2. The man's instructions were _____, so I did not know what to do.

3. The movie was a(n) _____ of the true story.

4. One role of the government is to _____ its people.

5. Politicians can appear to have _____ views when actually they do not.

Test

🎧 Listen to the conversation and take notes. **Track 2-30**

Man - Student	Woman - Newspaper Editor
• Has an _____ _____	• Thinks _____ _____
• Wrote about _____ _____ _____ _____ _____ _____	• Says the dean was _____ _____ _____ _____ _____ _____

Choose the correct answers. **Track 2-31**

1. What was the conversation mainly about?

(A) A discussion about whether or not an article could be published
(B) An argument about how good or bad the dean of the school was
(C) A request for advice on how to improve his newspaper article
(D) A demand that an article be written about the dean

2. Which of the following is true, according to the student?

(A) The dean is doing a terrible job at the school.
(B) His article is all about the good job the dean is doing at the school.
(C) What the dean did is morally ambiguous.
(D) The dean was famous for making the school worse.

3. Why does the newspaper editor say this: 🎧 ?

(A) To emphasize that she does not like the subject of the article that the student wrote
(B) To imply that writing anything bad about the school or its staff will get the student newspaper in trouble
(C) To encourage the student to write articles that will make people talk about them
(D) To find out what the student has written in his article

4. How does the student illustrate the idea that the dean has done something wrong?

(A) By mentioning that he is morally wrong
(B) By discussing the dean's policy regarding ethnic minorities
(C) By stating the lack of a legacy left by the dean
(D) By mentioning how students and staff feel about the dean

Lecture - Environment

Getting Ready to Listen

A. Learn the words.

Key Vocabulary

gravity	the force that causes something to fall to the ground
hydroelectricity	electricity produced by using water
drought	a long period of dry weather
dam	a wall built across a river to stop water from flowing
proven	tested and shown to be true or good

TOEFL® Vocabulary

annual	based on or calculated over a period of one year
convert	to change something into a different form
volume	the total amount of something
contrast	the difference between two things being compared
substitution	when someone or something is replaced by someone or something else

B. Learn the question type.

TOEFL® Question Type

Detail

How does the professor emphasize her point about X?

How does the professor define X?

Select the drawing/diagram that shows X?

- Incorrect answer choices may include information that is inaccurate or contradicts what the professor says.
- Incorrect answer choices may include similar-sounding words to those used by the professor but do not include the same information.

Practice

A. Listen to the first part of the lecture and choose the correct answers. `Track 2-32`

1. What is the main topic in this lecture?

   (A) Gravity
   (B) The differences between ways of generating power

2. What are the main topics in this lecture?

   (A) Hydroelectricity and tidal stream power
   (B) Gravity and rivers

3. How will the professor organize the lecture?

   (A) By categorizing information
   (B) By comparing and contrasting information

4. Choose the best note-taking diagram for this lecture.

   (A) Venn Diagram   (B) Categorizing Diagram   (C) Ordering Diagram

Note-taking

B. Draw the diagram chosen in question 4. Then insert the information from questions 1 and 2.

C. Now listen to the full lecture and complete your notes. `Track 2-33`

D. Choose the correct answers.

1. What is the lecture mainly about?

(A) The differences between hydroelectricity and tidal stream power

(B) Drought conditions in some parts of the world

2. According to the professor, what is one problem with hydroelectricity?

(A) It needs a running river so it can be affected by droughts.

(B) It is still being developed and has yet to be proven.

3. According to the professor, what is one problem with tidal stream electricity?

(A) It needs a running river so it can be affected by droughts.

(B) It is still being developed and has yet to be proven.

TOEFL® Vocabulary Practice

E. Fill in the blanks with the correct words.

annual	convert	contrast	volume	substitution

1. Large companies publish _____ reports for their stock holders.

2. If you travel to another country, you will need to _____ your money to its currency.

3. The _____ of dirt taken out of the hole filled three buckets.

4. During a sports game, if a player gets injured, coaches will make a(n) _____.

5. I like the _____ between light and dark colors in the painting.

Test

Listen to the lecture and take notes. `Track 2-34`

Water Power vs. Wind Power

- Location

- Cost

- Environment

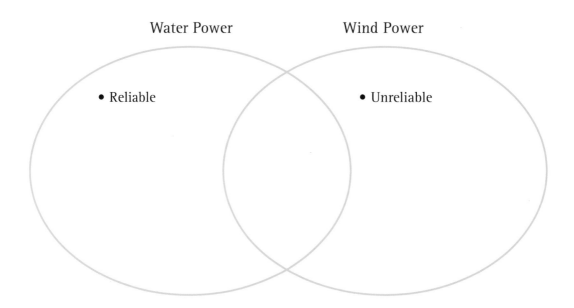

Water Power

Wind Power

- Reliable

- Unreliable

Choose the correct answers. `Track 2-35`

1. What is the main topic of the lecture?

(A) That wind and water power are the best ways to make power

(B) That wind power is more efficient than water power

(C) A comparison of wind power and water power

(D) The best sources of power

2. According to the professor, what is the main problem with water power?

   (A) It can only be produced near water.
   (B) Dams damage the environment.
   (C) It kills birds.
   (D) Both A and B

3. Why does the professor say this: ◯ ?

   (A) To show the differences between wind and water power
   (B) To show that wind and water power might be good alternative energy sources
   (C) To show that most energy sources are renewable
   (D) To show that wind and water power are the only renewable energy sources

4. What is the professor's opinion of the towers used to make wind power?

   (A) She admires the construction.
   (B) She thinks they are ugly.
   (C) She believes they are useful.
   (D) She claims they are more beautiful than dams.

5. Why does the professor discuss environmental concerns?

   (A) To point out the main reason people prefer wind power over water power
   (B) To help the student make the right choice about the best way to produce power
   (C) To highlight another similarity between wind power and water power
   (D) To clarify her preference for water power over wind power

6. What is likely to be true if someone has chosen to use water power instead of wind power?

   (A) The person thinks dams are better than wind towers.
   (B) The person enjoys fishing more than bird watching.
   (C) The person thinks birds need to be protected worldwide.
   (D) The person uses large amounts of electricity year round.

Check-up

A. Choose the correct answers.

1. When answering a conversation detail question
   (A) select the answer that explains the speaker's attitude toward the problem
   (B) choose the answer that includes a reason given by one of the speakers
   (C) select the answer that includes information not mentioned by the speakers
   (D) choose the answer that explains why a speaker asks a certain question

2. What should you do when answering a lecture detail question?
   (A) Choose the answer that best summarizes the professor's aim for giving the lecture.
   (B) Select an answer that includes similar-sounding words to those spoken by the professor.
   (C) Choose the answer that best represents the pattern to which the points of the lecture are presented.
   (D) Select an answer choice that includes the same information given by the speaker or speakers.

Key Vocabulary Practice

B. Fill in the blanks with the correct words.

gravity	hydroelectricity	drought	dam	merit
strive	proven	legacy	article	edition

1. _____ is more environmentally friendly than electricity made from coal.
2. Hydroelectricity has been _____ to work.
3. The force of _____ is weaker on the moon.
4. A(n) _____ is something built across a river to stop the flow of water.
5. A(n) _____ is a long period with no rain.
6. Professional athletes _____ to be the best at their sport.
7. The _____ on the front page of the newspaper was all about the new president.
8. Although the artist died over a century ago, her _____ of paintings and sculptures continue to be admired.
9. The first _____ of the book was worth a lot of money because so few were left.
10. Most of the new programs on TV don't have much _____ as far as I'm concerned.

94 | Listening |

[09] Conversation

Getting Ready to Listen

A. Learn the words.

Key Vocabulary

feedback	a response to something, intended to provide help for future development
admit	to acknowledge that something is true
relieved	feeling that a burden has been removed
address	to say something to somebody
occasionally	sometimes

TOEFL® Vocabulary

thesis	a lengthy academic paper
demonstrate	to show by doing
concise	short and clearly written or stated
insight	understanding; wisdom
assessment	a method of looking at student performance, like an exam

B. Learn the question type.

TOEFL® Question Type

Function

What does the student imply when he/she says this: 🎧 ?

Why does the student say this: 🎧 ?

You will hear part of the conversation again.

• Incorrect answer choices may suggest reasons not supported by the words spoken in the conversation.

• Incorrect answer choices may have reasons contradictory to the intonation of the speaker's voice.

Practice

A. Listen to the first part of the conversation and choose the correct answers.

Track 2-36

1. What do the speakers mainly discuss?

    (A) The professor gives the student feedback for his thesis.

    (B) The professor explains to the student how to write a thesis.

2. How does the student feel when he begins speaking with the professor?

    (A) Confident and relaxed

    (B) Somewhat nervous

Note-taking

B. Listen to the full conversation and take notes. Track 2-37

Man - Student	Woman - Professor
• Is going for _____ _____	• Thought the thesis was _____ _____
• Has been _____ _____	• Noticed a few _____ _____
• Wrote about _____ _____	• Says most ideas were _____

C. Choose the correct answers.

1. Why does the professor say this: ◯ ? **Track 2-38**

(A) To reassure the student that even with some mistakes, it was a good paper

(B) To tell the student that his thesis was perfect

2. The professor mentions spelling mistakes in order to make the student realize that

(A) They are easy to correct but will make him lose marks if missed.

(B) He is not a good writer and will not receive a good mark.

3. Which of the following is true, according to the student?

(A) He finished his thesis early and had a lot of time to look over it.

(B) He ran out of time toward the deadline and could not check it properly.

TOEFL® Vocabulary Practice

D. Fill in the blanks with the correct words.

thesis	demonstrate	concise	assessment	insights

1. Most courses have some kind of _____ to test how the students are performing.

2. Other students may have different _____ that they can bring to the class discussion.

3. In order to graduate from college, students often have to write a(n) _____.

4. It is often better to _____ how to do something rather than just explain it.

5. When writing a short article, journalists must be _____ with their writing.

Test

Listen to the conversation and take notes. **Track 2-39**

Woman - Student	Man - Professor
• Has finished _____ _____	• Says it is not always good _____ _____
• Would like _____	• Says the student has _____
• Has done a lot of _____	_____

Choose the correct answers. **Track 2-40**

1. Why does the student visit the professor?

(A) She would like to submit an essay she has written.
(B) She would like some advice on what to write for her thesis.
(C) She would like him to look over an essay she has written and give advice.
(D) She needs to tell him that she will not be able to hand in her essay on time.

2. What resulted from the professor looking over the student's essay draft?

(A) She will make some small changes to the paper and then submit it.
(B) She is required to change the subject of the essay and start again.
(C) The student was able to submit the essay without making any changes.
(D) The student will make a lot of changes to the paper before it is submitted.

3. What does the woman imply when she says this: ◯?

(A) She is worried that she has not done enough preparation for the essay.
(B) She thinks that she did not need to do any research before writing the paper.
(C) She believes that she has done enough research but wrote the paper quickly.
(D) She is confident that she has done a lot of research and has written a good paper.

4. According to the professor, why was the student's essay impressive?

(A) The first part of the essay was well written, but the ideas became side-tracked sometimes.
(B) The student did exactly what was asked and the paper was concise and well written.
(C) The student made no spelling mistakes in the entire essay.
(D) The essay was completed very quickly.

98 | Listening |

Lecture - Psychology

Getting Ready to Listen

A. Learn the words.

Key Vocabulary

psychoanalysis	a method of psychology that tries to explain behavior as a result of thoughts we are not aware of
behaviorism	a school of psychology that explains behavior as a result of rewards and punishment
reasoning	the process of thinking carefully about something in order to make a judgment
school	an opinion or way of thinking about something, shared by many people
value	an idea about what is right and wrong, or what is important

TOEFL® Vocabulary

ideology	a set of beliefs that influence the way people behave
overlap	to include some but not all of the same things
depression	a mental condition of being unhappy
intelligence	the ability to learn, understand, and think about things
cognitive	related to the process of knowing, understanding, and learning something

B. Learn the question type.

TOEFL® Question Type

Function
What is the purpose of the professor's/student's response?
What does the professor imply when he/she says this: ◯ ?

You will hear part of the lecture again.

- Incorrect answer choices may contain reasons not supported by the words spoken by the professor.
- Incorrect answer choices may contain explanations that cannot be inferred from the logical flow of the lecture.
- Incorrect answer choices may contain explanations that cannot be inferred from the professor's tone of voice.

Practice

A. **Listen to the first part of the lecture and choose the correct answers.** `Track 2-41`

1. What is the main topic in this lecture?

   (A) Schools of psychology   (B) Psychoanalysis

2. What are the key points in this lecture?

   (A) How the schools differ

   (B) How one school came out of another school

3. How does the professor describe the main topic?

   (A) By providing theories and evidence to support it

   (B) By listing people who had important ideas

4. Choose the best note-taking diagram for this lecture.

   (A) Concept Defining   (B) Cause and Effect   (C) Theory and Evidence
       Diagram   Diagram   Diagram

Note-taking

B. **Draw the diagram chosen in question 4. Then insert the information from questions 1 and 2.**

C. **Now listen to the full lecture and complete your notes.** `Track 2-42`

D. Choose the correct answers.

1. Why does the professor say this: ⌒ ? `Track 2-43`

(A) To give an example

(B) To introduce a new theory

2. What does the professor mean when she says this: ⌒ ? `Track 2-44`

(A) That people do things because they are afraid of punishment

(B) That people do things because of their values

3. What is behaviorism?

(A) A school of thought that says people do things because of rewards and punishment

(B) A school of thought that says people do things because of our reasoning and thinking

TOEFL® Vocabulary Practice

E. Fill in the blanks with the correct words.

ideology	overlapped	depression	intelligence	cognitive

1. The _____ of our modern culture is very different today than it was just 100 years ago.

2. An IQ test is a test of someone's _____.

3. _____ is a mental illness that makes people feel very sad.

4. Someone with a brain injury may lose _____ abilities.

5. The time that Bush and Blair were both heads of state _____ by several years.

Test

Listen to the lecture and take notes. **Track 2-45**

Neuro-chips

- Brain
- Nerves
- Depression

Problem	Solution
Damaged brain	
	Neuro-chip placed in brain to make parts work better

Choose the correct answers. **Track 2-46**

1. What is the main topic of the lecture?

(A) Brain injuries

(B) Neuro-chips and supercomputers

(C) Neuro-chips used in the brain

(D) The development of neuro-chips

2. According to the professor, what is one way that a neuro-chip could help someone with a damaged brain?

(A) Make them more comfortable
(B) Restore cognitive functioning
(C) Restore muscles in the legs
(D) Make them more intelligent

3. Why does the professor say this: 🎧 ?

(A) Because neuro chips are like a movie
(B) Because neuro-chips have many potential uses
(C) Because neuro-chips are new
(D) Because neuro-chips will make better computers

4. How does the professor feel about neuro-chips?

(A) Interested
(B) Curious
(C) Excited
(D) Skeptical

5. Why does the professor mention computers?

(A) Neuro-chips will make people think like computers.
(B) Computers are a possible use of neuro-chips.
(C) Computers are made with neuro-chips.
(D) Neuro-chips and computers are the same thing.

6. What can be inferred about neuro-chips?

(A) They will make people smarter.
(B) They will be in our computer soon.
(C) They will need more research before they are used.
(D) They are expensive.

Check-up

A. Choose the correct answers.

1. When answering a conversation function question
   (A) choose the answer that best explains the speakers' tone of voice
   (B) choose the answer that best explains the problem the student wants solved
   (C) choose the answer that conveys information not mentioned or suggested by the speakers
   (D) choose the answer that puts the steps in a sequence in the correct order

2. What should you do when answering a lecture function question?
   (A) Select the answer that best contradicts the main idea of the lecture.
   (B) Pick the answer that best explains the intonation used by the professor.
   (C) Select the answer that includes the most minor details from the lecture.
   (D) Pick the answer that most logically suggests what the professor will discuss next.

Key Vocabulary Practice

B. Fill in the blanks with the correct words.

psychoanalysis	behaviorism	reasoning	schools	occasionally
value	feedback	admit	relieved	address

1. _____ explains human behavior by examining rewards and punishment.
2. There are four _____ of psychology.
3. _____ explains human behavior by examining thoughts that the person may not be aware of.
4. Philosophers use _____ skills to solve problems.
5. Most people share the _____ that it is wrong to lie.
6. The criminal would not _____ having robbed the store.
7. In the meeting, the manager did not _____ the new timetable.
8. _____, I like to eat pizza.
9. The man was _____ when he found his car keys under the table.
10. When a student writes a thesis, he will often receive _____ from a teacher to improve his writing.

[10] Conversation

Getting Ready to Listen

A. Learn the words.

Key Vocabulary

slight	small in size, degree, amount, or importance
distracted	showing a lack of concentration
lag	to progress more slowly so as to fall behind
warranted	deserving; worthy to receive
deficit	the amount by which a total is less than it should be

TOEFL® Vocabulary

practitioner	someone who practices a profession
passive	tending not to participate actively in something
scope	range in which something operates
empirical	based on observation and experiment instead of theory
intermediate	lying or occurring between two different points, forms, or extremes

B. Learn the question type.

TOEFL® Question Type

Attitude

What is the man's/woman's attitude toward X?

What can be inferred from the man's/woman's response?

• Incorrect answers may provide inferences unrelated to the conversation.

• Incorrect answers may suggest attitudes based on the literal words spoken rather than on the tone of voice.

Practice

A. Listen to the first part of the conversation and choose the correct answers.

Track 3-1

1. What is the main topic in this lecture?

   (A) The student is describing problems that he has had at home.

   (B) The student is asking if he can do anything to gain extra credit in class.

2. How does the professor explain why the student's credit in class has been so low?

   (A) She mentions how he has been distracted.

   (B) She shows him his exam results from the rest of the year.

Note-taking

B. Listen to the full conversation and take notes. Track 3-2

Man - Student	Woman - Professor
• Is worried _____	• Has a _____
• Asks if _____	• Says the student has _____
• Has had _____	• Is glad that _____

C. Choose the correct answers.

1. What is the professor's opinion of the student's lack of credit?

(A) She is glad that the student realized that it is a problem before it is too late.

(B) She is angry that the student has been distracted from his work in class.

2. What is the student's attitude toward gaining extra credit?

(A) He is frustrated that he will have to do extra work in order to get credit.

(B) He is hopeful that there is something that he can do in order to get credit.

3. Why does the student say this: ( ) ? **Track 3-3**

(A) To emphasize that his problems are over and he will work hard from now on

(B) To explain to the professor that he has a passive personality and does not like to be pushed

TOEFL® Vocabulary Practice

D. Fill in the blanks with the correct words.

| practitioner | passive | scope | empirical | intermediate |

1. A scientific fact is a theory that has been proven in _____ experiments.

2. You've done extensive research, but much of it is beyond the _____ of the essay topic.

3. The football team lost because their best players were too _____ on the field.

4. The students were grouped into three skill levels; low, _____, and high.

5. Another name for a doctor is a medical _____.

Test

Listen to the conversation and take notes. **Track 3-4**

Woman - Student	Man - Professor
• Would like _____ _____ • Has _____ _____ _____ _____ _____ _____ _____ _____ _____	• Says that her request had better ___ _____ • Understands that _____ _____ _____ _____ _____ _____ _____ _____ _____

Choose the correct answers. **Track 3-5**

1. Why does the student go to see her professor?

(A) To request extra work in return for extra credit in her class

(B) To apply for work in the field of science

(C) To ask for an extra week to write a paper she is doing for extra credit

(D) To complain that she has too much work to do that week

2. What resulted from the conversation between the student and professor?

(A) The student was given one more week to complete her paper.

(B) The professor decided that the student had failed the class.

(C) The student was told to complete the exams and paper in the same week.

(D) The professor explained to the student that she had all the credit she needed.

3. What was the professor's attitude toward the student's problem?

(A) He was excited that she was working hard to better her grades.

(B) He was frustrated that the student had repeatedly become distracted.

(C) He was worried that the student was working too hard.

(D) He was angry that the student hadn't finished her paper earlier.

4. How did the student organize the information about what she wanted from the professor?

(A) She explained that she had a number of exams and then asked for the extra week.

(B) She told the professor that she could lag further behind and asked for extra time.

(C) She asked for an extra week and then told the professor about her exams.

(D) She told the professor that she is working extra hard and then asked for another week to complete the paper.

Lecture - Technology

Getting Ready to Listen

A. Learn the words.

Key Vocabulary

drum	a large round container
magnetic	having the power of a magnet
ceramic	made from baked clay
obsolete	no longer useful, because something better now exists
semiconductor	a substance that allows electric currents to pass through it

TOEFL® Vocabulary

analogous	similar to another situation or thing so that a comparison can be made
manual	involving working with one's hands or physical strength
chronological	arranged according to when things happened or were made
sequence	the order that something happens
norm	the usual or normal situation

B. Learn the question type.

TOEFL® Question Type

Attitude

What is the professor's point of view concerning X?

What does the professor mean when he/she says this: ◯ ?

- Incorrect answers may provide inferences unrelated to the lecture.
- Incorrect answers may suggest attitudes based on the literal words spoken rather than on the tone of voice.

Practice

A. Listen to the first part of the lecture and choose the correct answers. `Track 3-6`

1. What is the main topic of this lecture?
    (A) Computer memory
    (B) Types of computers today

2. What are the key points of this lecture?
    (A) Human memory, manual system, and sequence memory
    (B) Drum memory, magnetic core memory, and semiconductor memory

3. How does the professor describe the main topic?
    (A) By discussing each category in turn
    (B) By presenting problems and their solutions

4. Choose the best note-taking diagram for this lecture.

| (A) Categorizing Diagram | (B) Problem and Solution Diagram | (C) Concept Defining Diagram |

Note-taking

B. Draw the diagram chosen in question 4. Then insert the information from questions 1 and 2.

C. Now listen to the full lecture and complete your notes. `Track 3-7`

D. Choose the correct answers.

1. What does the professor mean when he says this: ( ) ? `Track 3-8`

    (A) Our computers don't work well, so that means they must have good memory.

    (B) To work well, computers need a lot of memory.

2. What is the professor's opinion of the manual computer made in 1834?

    (A) He doesn't think it worked well.

    (B) He is surprised it isn't still used today.

3. What can be inferred from the student's response? ( ) `Track 3-9`

    (A) She is surprised by that information.

    (B) She thinks the professor is wrong.

TOEFL® Vocabulary Practice

E. Fill in the blanks with the correct words.

analogous	manual	chronological	sequence	norm

1. Timelines are arranged in _____ order.

2. In America, it is the _____ to begin school when you are five years old.

3. If you see a movie out of _____, it is hard to understand.

4. The Technology Revolution of today is _____ to the Industrial Revolution of 200 years ago.

5. Construction is a form of _____ labor.

Test

Listen to the lecture and take notes. **Track 3-10**

Nanocomputers

- Electronic
- Chemical
- Mechanical
- Quantum

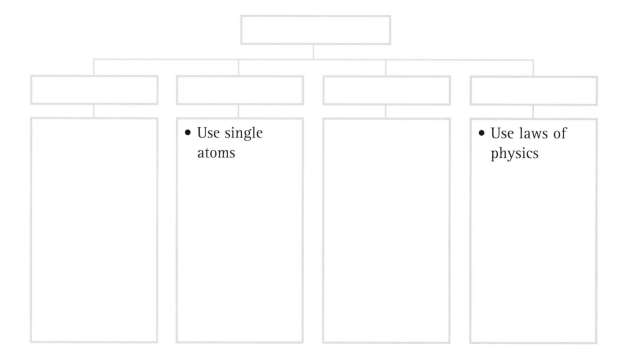

- Use single atoms

- Use laws of physics

Choose the correct answers. **Track 3-11**

1. What is the main topic of the lecture?

(A) How nanocomputers could be made
(B) Possible uses of nanorobots
(C) Possible types of nanocomputers
(D) The fastest computer ever made

2. According to the professor, how could mechanical nanocomputers be used?

(A) To control nanorobots

(B) To build nanorobots

(C) To attack diseases

(D) To build faster computers

3. Why does the professor say this: ( ) ?

(A) Because the student misunderstood

(B) To explain what nanocomputers are

(C) To teach the meaning of the word

(D) To explain the uses of nanotechnology

4. What is the professor's opinion of quantum nanocomputers?

(A) He thinks they are the most exciting.

(B) He doesn't think they will work.

(C) He thinks they will be too fast.

(D) He thinks they are too complicated.

5. Why does the professor discuss cancer?

(A) To show how nanocomputers could infect a computer network

(B) To show how nanorobots could cure diseases

(C) To show how chemical nanocomputers would work

(D) To show how mechanical nanocomputers would work

6. What can be inferred about quantum nanocomputers?

(A) They may be the most useful.

(B) They may be developed first.

(C) They may be the hardest to develop.

(D) They may never be developed.

Check-up

A. Choose the correct answers.

1. When answering a conversation attitude question
   - (A) listen for emotion expressed in the tone of the speakers' voices
   - (B) listen for the sequence of steps to understand the speakers' emotions
   - (C) listen to the volume of the speakers' voices to understand the main idea
   - (D) listen for repeated content words or phrases to understand the speakers' purpose

2. What should you do when answering a lecture attitude question?
   - (A) Choose the answer that best explains the professor's tone of voice.
   - (B) Select the answer that puts the steps of a sequence into the correct order.
   - (C) Choose the answer that best represents the pattern to which the points of the lecture are presented.
   - (D) Select the answer that best contradicts the main idea of the lecture.

Key Vocabulary Practice

B. Fill in the blanks with the correct words.

drum	magnetic	ceramic	obsolete	semiconductor
slight	distracted	lag	deficit	warranted

1. A compass points to _____ north.
2. The invention of the automobile made horse and buggies _____.
3. My cell phone, digital camera, and computer all have a(n) _____ in them.
4. Sometimes, water or oil is stored in a barrel or _____.
5. Many cups and plates are _____.
6. He was trying to study, but the music _____ him.
7. The child was not tall enough to go on the fairground ride by a(n) _____ amount.
8. A visit to the doctor's office was _____ because his son had a high fever.
9. As the race went on, the slow runners began to _____ behind the leaders.
10. The _____ in the charity fund was caused by people paying their donations late.

[11] Conversation

Getting Ready to Listen

A. Learn the words.

Key Vocabulary

plagiarize	to take something that someone else has written or thought and try to pass it off as original work of your own
degree	an amount of something
instruction	spoken or written information on how to do something
handbook	a reference book
passage	a section of a piece of writing

TOEFL® Vocabulary

repercussion	something that results from an action, usually a consequence
publication	an item that has been published
quote	to copy the exact words, spoken or written, of a person while giving him or her credit for it
cite	to acknowledge the use of somebody's work
suspension	a temporary leave from a team, organization, or school especially as a punishment

B. Learn the question type.

TOEFL® Question Type

Organization

How does the man/woman organize information about X?

Why does the man/woman discuss X?

Why does the man/woman mention X?

• Organization questions are more commonly asked after lectures rather than conversations.

• Incorrect answer choices may suggest inaccurate connections between parts of the conversation.

Practice

A. **Listen to the first part of the conversation and choose the correct answers.**
   Track 3-12

1. What is the main topic in this lecture?

   (A) A student being accused of plagiarism
   (B) A student wanting to understand plagiarism

2. How does the professor address what the student has done?

   (A) By directly asking the student if he knows about his copied work from the Internet
   (B) By talking about another student in the class who plagiarized material

Note-taking

B. **Listen to the full conversation and take notes.**   Track 3-13

Woman - Professor	Man - Student
• Her concern is _____ _____ _____ _____ • Takes plagiarism _____ • Says he copied _____ _____ _____ _____ _____	• Used the Internet but _____ _____ • Wants to take _____ _____ _____ _____ _____ _____ _____ _____

C. Choose the correct answers.

1. Why does the professor mention the Internet?

    (A) The student's assignment was posted on the Internet.

    (B) The student copied work from the Internet.

2. How did the professor organize the information about the student's plagiarizing?

    (A) She discussed a past case of plagiarism and then talked about his paper.

    (B) She asked him about his actions and then explained the repercussions of his actions.

3. What can be inferred from the student's response? Track 3-14

    (A) He is nervous.   (B) He is sad.

TOEFL® Vocabulary Practice

D. Fill in the blanks with the correct words.

repercussion	publication	quote	cite	suspension

1. The consequence of missing five of the ten meetings is _____ from the speech club.

2. It is a good idea to _____ other authors as a way of supporting your argument.

3. The student used many resources to write his paper and had to _____ all of their names at the end.

4. The _____ of not completing the final project is a failing grade in the class.

5. Next month, the school will put out a _____ about all the sports teams.

Test

Listen to the conversation and take notes.　**Track 3-15**

Man - Student	Woman - Professor
• Is reading the _____ _____ _____ _____ _____ _____ _____ _____	• Says all students could benefit from _____ _____ • Is glad to know _____ _____ _____ • Says plagiarism is _____ _____ _____ _____

Choose the correct answers.　**Track 3-16**

1. What is the main topic of the conversation?

    (A) The Writing Center
    (B) The student handbook
    (C) Plagiarism
    (D) A research project

2. What can be inferred from the student's response when he says this: 🎧 ?

    (A) He is excited.
    (B) He wants to avoid being accused of plagiarism.
    (C) He is still confused about what plagiarism is.
    (D) He is not interested in the conversation anymore.

3. Why does the professor mention the repercussions of plagiarism?

    (A) To express the seriousness of plagiarism
    (B) To imply that the student has plagiarized
    (C) To express her interest in the topic of plagiarism
    (D) To correct an incorrect idea that the student has

4. According to the professor, what should the student do if he is in doubt as to whether or not he is plagiarizing?

    (A) Call a professor
    (B) Cite or quote the original author
    (C) Start over
    (D) Don't worry about it

Lecture - Civics and Government

Getting Ready to Listen

A. Learn the words.

Key Vocabulary

NATO	North Atlantic Treaty Organization; a military alliance formed by countries in North America and Europe as a pact to defend each other
alliance	an arrangement in which two or more countries, groups, etc. agree to work together
conventional	used for a long time and considered usual
assure	to make something certain to happen
redefine	to give a new or different definition

TOEFL® Vocabulary

seek	to try to achieve or get something
participation	the act of taking part in an activity or event
outcome	the final result
mutual	shared; common
albeit	though

B. Learn the question type.

TOEFL® Question Type

Organization

How does the professor organize the information about X that he/she presents to the class?

How does the professor illustrate X?

Why does the professor discuss X?

- Incorrect answer choices may provide unconnected reasons for a specific action by the professor.
- Incorrect answer choices may suggest incorrect order to, or connections between, parts of the lecture.

Practice

A. Listen to the first part of the lecture and choose the correct answers. `Track 3-17`

1. What is the main topic of this lecture?
   (A) The formation and purpose of NATO
   (B) The formation and purpose of the Treaty of Brussels

2. What are the key points of this lecture?
   (A) The Treaty of Brussels, the Western European Union, and Article 5
   (B) The steps leading to the formation of NATO, including the Treaty of Brussels, and the purpose of NATO

3. How does the professor describe the main topic?
   (A) By presenting the information in the order it occurred
   (B) By categorizing the information

4. Choose the best note-taking diagram for this lecture.
   (A) Cause and Effect Diagram   (B) Concept Defining Diagram   (C) Ordering Diagram

`Note-taking`

B. Draw the diagram chosen in question 4. Then insert the information from questions 1 and 2.

C. Now listen to the full lecture and complete your notes. `Track 3-18`

D. Choose the correct answers.

1. What is the professor's opinion of NATO?

(A) He thinks it is less important than the Treaty of Brussels.

(B) He thinks it is an important organization.

2. Why does the professor mention the Treaty of Brussels?

(A) Because he thinks it was more important than NATO

(B) Because it was signed before NATO formed

3. Why does the professor discuss Article 5?

(A) Because it was at the heart of NATO

(B) Because it states all sides will defend the USSR

TOEFL® Vocabulary Practice

E. Fill in the blanks with the correct words.

| sought | participation | outcome | mutual | albeit |

1. It is only the first half of the game. The _____ is still unknown.

2. One third of my grade is based on class _____.

3. _____ consent means that both people agree.

4. Columbus _____ to find a trade route to Asia.

5. The movie was quite funny, _____ not very realistic.

Test

Listen to the lecture and take notes. **Track 3-19**

History of the Warsaw Pact

• NATO

• Hungary & Czechoslovakia

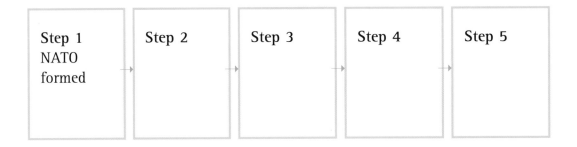

Step 1 NATO formed	Step 2	Step 3	Step 4	Step 5

Choose the correct answers. **Track 3-20**

1. What is the main topic of the lecture?

(A) The relationship between NATO and the WARSAW Pact nations
(B) The history of the WARSAW Pact
(C) The history of the USSR
(D) The invasions of Hungary and Czechoslovakia

2. What happened in 1968?

(A) Hungary was invaded.
(B) Czechoslovakia was invaded.
(C) Warsaw Pact was formed.
(D) NATO was formed.

122 | Listening |

3. What does the professor imply when he says this: ⌒ ?

    (A) This was common.

    (B) This is surprising.

    (C) This didn't happen.

    (D) This is common knowledge.

4. What is the professor's attitude toward the invasion of Hungary?

    (A) The USSR was taking a necessary step.

    (B) There was no way Hungary could win.

    (C) He doubts people in the USSR knew about it.

    (D) He believes there were both good and bad results.

5. How did the professor organize the information about the Warsaw Pact?

    (A) Cause and effect

    (B) Categorization

    (C) Chronologically

    (D) Problems and solutions

6. What can be inferred about the end of the Warsaw Pact?

    (A) It was a sad day.

    (B) It ended around the same time NATO ended.

    (C) Many people were happy.

    (D) It has not ended.

Check-up

A. Choose the correct answers.

1. When answering a conversation organization question
   (A) choose the answer that explains the main problem the student wants solved
   (B) select the answer that best contradicts the main idea of the lecture
   (C) choose the answer that connects different parts of the conversation
   (D) select the answer that best explains an idiom or expression used by the speakers

2. What should you do when answering a lecture organization question?
   (A) Choose the answer that best explains the speaker's emotions about the topic.
   (B) Select the answer that includes the most minor details from the lecture.
   (C) Choose the answer that is most consistent with the professor's tone of voice.
   (D) Select the answer that best represents the pattern to which the points of the lecture are presented.

Key Vocabulary Practice

B. Fill in the blanks with the correct words.

NATO	alliance	redefined	conventional	assure
plagiarize	degree	instruction	handbook	passage

1. I can _____ you that flying is safe.

2. The US, Canada, and most of Western Europe formed a military alliance called _____.

3. My friend likes to read newspapers on the Internet, but I prefer the _____ paper edition.

4. During World War II the US and USSR formed a(n) _____ to defeat Germany.

5. The word "surfing" has been _____ from something you do on the ocean to something you do on the Internet.

6. The students were asked to read a certain _____ and write a summary of what they read.

7. The university encourages students not to _____ by giving them resources to help them.

8. A(n) _____ is given to every new employee to teach the guidelines.

9. A(n) _____ sheet is passed out to the students before the research project is assigned.

10. To a certain _____, the students liked working on the final project.

[12] Conversation

Getting Ready to Listen

A. Learn the words.

Key Vocabulary

in regards to	relating to
adjoining	attached to
intramural	only involving the members of a single school instead of members from various colleges
propose	to put something forward; to suggest a course of action
peak	the highest point of activity, intensity, or strength

TOEFL® Vocabulary

facility	something built or established to serve a particular purpose
valid	having a solid justification
site	an area of land; a location
committee	a group of people chosen to represent a larger group
commence	to begin

B. Learn the question type.

TOEFL® Question Type

Content

What is the likely outcome of doing X then Y?

What does the man/woman imply about X?

Indicate whether each of the following was mentioned in the conversation.

- Questions asking for information to be organized into a table are more common after lectures.
- Incorrect answer choices may include inferences not supported by the speakers' words or attitude.
- Incorrect answer choices may include past actions or conditions instead of probable future actions or conditions.

Practice

A. **Listen to the first part of the conversation and choose the correct answers.**
Track 3-21

1. What is the main topic in this lecture?
   (A) Getting the hours changed for the recreation center and snack bar
   (B) The meeting the student had with the Sites and Facility Committee

2. How does the student explain what she is trying to get changed?
   (A) By talking about the benefits for the recreation facility.
   (B) By listing exactly what she wants.

Note-taking

B. **Listen to the full conversation and take notes.** Track 3-22

Woman - Student	Man - University Employee
• Wants to talk about _____ _____	• Is able to _____ _____
• Says the recreation area opens _____ _____	• Says they meet _____ _____
• Wants the recreation facility open _____ _____ _____ _____ _____	_____ _____ _____ _____ _____

C. Choose the correct answers.

1. What is the likely outcome if the student meets with the committee as opposed to just meeting with Mr. Kovach?

(A) She has a better chance of getting the hours changed.

(B) She may not be able to use the facilities at all.

2. Why does the woman mention the students with evening classes?

(A) They would benefit from the recreation facility being open later.

(B) They use the snack bar in the evening.

3. According to the student, what would happen if the snack bar were to open during peak hours?

(A) It would increase use of the recreation area.

(B) It would make money.

TOEFL® Vocabulary Practice

D. Fill in the blanks with the correct words.

facility	valid	site	committee	commence

1. The _____ of the new library is located downtown.

2. The professor requires _____ reasons if a student wants to miss class.

3. The main responsibility of a donation _____ is to raise money for the school.

4. After lunch, the meeting will _____ in the main meeting hall.

5. Behind the dorms is where the recreation _____ is located.

Test

⌒ Listen to the conversation and take notes.　**Track 3-23**

Woman - University Employee	Man - Student
• Heard _____ _____ _____ • Is interested in _____ _____ _____ _____	• Says it took a long _____ _____ • Gave them _____ _____ • Was very _____ • Wants to host _____ _____ _____

Choose the correct answers.　**Track 3-24**

1. What is the main topic of the conversation?

(A) The athletic team's spring schedule
(B) The permission given to use the courtyard for concerts
(C) The new site for spring activities
(D) The purpose of the Site and Facilities Committee

2. What resulted from the conversation about the Student Activities Club?

(A) The woman recommended a different employee to be a sponsor.
(B) The woman volunteered to sponsor the Student Activities Club.
(C) The student arranged another meeting with the committee.
(D) The student lost track of time and was late for class.

3. What is the university employee's attitude about being a sponsor?

(A) Not interested
(B) Excited
(C) Passive
(D) Apprehensive

4. What can be inferred from the student's response when the university employee tells him she is interested in being the sponsor?

(A) He is nervous.
(B) He is shocked.
(C) He is excited.
(D) He is doubtful.

Lecture - Theater

Getting Ready to Listen

A. Learn the words.

Key Vocabulary

approach	a method of doing something
scene	a part of a play during which there is no change in time or place
innocence	the state of not being guilty of a crime
method acting	an acting technique where actors draw on their own emotions and reactions
situation	the occurrences and the conditions at a particular time and place

TOEFL® Vocabulary

intensity	strength of feelings or opinions; seriousness
display	to show
dramatic	exciting or impressive
inhibition	a feeling of shyness or embarrassment that prevents one from doing something
transformation	a complete change in someone or something

B. Learn the question type.

TOEFL® Question Type

Content

In the lecture, the professor describes X. Indicate whether each of the following is mentioned. Based on information in the lecture, indicate whether each sentence below describes X, Y, or Z. What does the professor imply about X?

• Questions asking for information to be organized into a table are more common after lectures.
• Incorrect answer choices may contain words that sound similar to those mentioned in the lecture but were not actually mentioned.
• Incorrect answer choices may include connections between parts of the lecture that are not supported by the lecture.

Practice

A. **Listen to the first part of the lecture and choose the correct answers.** `Track 3-25`

1. What is the main topic of this lecture?

    (A) Method acting

    (B) The history of acting

2. What are the key points of this lecture?

    (A) The different schools of method acting

    (B) Acting styles

3. How does the professor describe the main topic?

    (A) By explaining the result of applying certain method acting techniques

    (B) By comparing and contrasting certain aspects of method acting

4. Choose the best note-taking diagram for this lecture.

    (A) Venn Diagram   (B) Technique and Result   (C) Ordering Diagram

`Note-taking`

B. **Draw the diagram chosen in question 4. Then insert the information from questions 1 and 2.**

C. **Now listen to the full lecture and complete your notes.** `Track 3-26`

D. Choose the correct answers.

1. Why does the professor mention the Actors' Studio?

    (A) Because all actors go there

    (B) Because it is the most well-known method acting school

2. What can be inferred about emotions?

    (A) It is easy for actors to show emotion.

    (B) Actors want to show a lot of emotions.

3. What is the likely outcome of remembering past emotions when acting?

    (A) You will have difficulty remembering your lines.

    (B) You will show those emotions when acting.

TOEFL® Vocabulary Practice

E. Fill in the blanks with the correct words.

intensity	display	dramatic	inhibitions	transformation

1. The goal scored in the last second of the game made a _____ end to the game.

2. Art galleries have paintings on _____.

3. A caterpillar makes a _____ into a butterfly.

4. Your _____ can keep you from trying new things.

5. The _____ of the light made it difficult to see.

Test

🎧 Listen to the lecture and take notes. `Track 3-27`

Viewpoints

- Space
- Shape
- Time
- Movement

Cause	Effect

- Some acting teachers thought

  _____
  _____
  _____
  _____
  _____
  _____
  _____
  _____
  _____
  _____

→

→

Choose the correct answers. `Track 3-28`

1. What is the main topic of the lecture?

   (A) Method acting
   (B) Theory of dance
   (C) The viewpoints approach to acting
   (D) Movement in acting

2. What are the four viewpoints?

    (A) Strength, time, place, shape

    (B) Space, shape, time, movement

    (C) Space, shape, place, movement

    (D) Space, shape, time, place

3. Why does the professor say this: 🎧 ?

    (A) To clarify the student's question

    (B) So the student would listen

    (C) To correct the student

    (D) To show that the student was correct

4. What is the professor's opinion of viewpoints?

    (A) Positive

    (B) Negative

    (C) Curious

    (D) Skeptical

5. Why does the professor discuss acting and emotions?

    (A) Because viewpoints teaches parts of acting that weren't emotional

    (B) Because emotions are the most important part of acting

    (C) Because emotions aren't important in acting

    (D) Because viewpoints teaches emotion and acting

6. What can be inferred about actors who use viewpoints?

    (A) They will use other methods to show emotion.

    (B) They will show no emotion when they are acting.

    (C) They show more emotion than other actors do.

    (D) They show less emotion than other actors do.

Check-up

A. Choose the correct answers.

1. When answering a conversation content question
   (A) select the answer that provides an inference based on both the speakers' words and tone
   (B) select the answer choice that demonstrates why the speaker asks a rhetorical question
   (C) select the answer that contains the most minor details mentioned in the conversation
   (D) select the answer choice that explains the main problem the students want solved

2. What should you do when answering a lecture content question?
   (A) Pick the answer that gives an inference not supported by the professor's words or tone.
   (B) Choose the answer that includes similar-sounding words to those used by the professor.
   (C) Pick the answer that contradicts the steps of a process mentioned in the lecture.
   (D) Choose the answer that provides the most logical connection between the parts of the lecture.

Key Vocabulary Practice

B. Fill in the blanks with the correct words.

approach	peak	propose	method acting	situation
in regards to	adjoining	intramural	innocence	scenes

1. Having no money is a difficult _____.
2. Method acting is one _____ to teaching acting.
3. Many people accused of crimes try to prove their _____.
4. _____ is a popular way to teach acting.
5. In the movie *Harry Potter*, many of the _____ take place at Hogwarts.
6. The student arranged a meeting with his professor _____ the final project.
7. The _____ volleyball games are held in the evening.
8. We can meet at the library and have lunch in the _____ coffee shop.
9. Lunch time is usually the _____ hours of operation for the local sandwich shop.
10. Students often _____ different due dates for their final projects to be due.

[Review 2]

Conversation 1

🎧 **Listen to the conversation and take notes.** `Track 3-29`

Woman - Student	Man - Professor
• Says she will _____	• Says it would be _____
• Asks if professor can _____	• Says it will be _____
• Says she is _____	• Locates _____
• Hopes she will _____	• Asks what type of _____
• Gives professor _____	_____
_____	_____
_____	_____
_____	_____
_____	_____
_____	_____

Choose the correct answers. `Track 3-30`

1. What is the main topic of the conversation?

(A) The student wants to ask her professor for a recommendation, but is too shy.

(B) The professor is recommending that the student attend graduate school.

(C) The student is asking her professor to write her a recommendation.

(D) The student is unlikely to attend graduate school because she doesn't have a recommendation.

2. According to the student, why does she want the professor to write her a recommendation?

(A) Because she can't write it herself

(B) Because she is applying for a summer internship

(C) Because she wants to attend graduation

(D) Because she is applying to graduate school

3. What can be inferred from the student's response: 🎧 ?

(A) The student is embarrassed by the professor's comment.

(B) The student is annoyed with the professor's comment.

(C) The student is angry with the professor's comment.

(D) The student is unhappy with the professor's comment.

4. What does the professor mean when he says this: 🎧 ?

(A) Often when he writes recommendations, people expect him to lie for them.

(B) Often when he writes recommendations, he makes comments that may not be true.

(C) Usually when he writes recommendations, he is paid for his services.

(D) Usually when he writes recommendations, he is not asked in advance.

Listen to the lecture and take notes. Track 3-31

Things you can do to live a long life

- don't smoke

- eat fruit

- exercise

- get regular sleep

Things you shouldn't do:
- smoke

Things you should eat/drink:

Exercise:

Choose the correct answers. Track 3-32

1. What is the main topic of the lecture?
   (A) How to live a good life
   (B) How to be healthy
   (C) How to live a long life
   (D) How to avoid heart disease

2. According to the professor, how does refined sugar affect the body's cells?

    (A) It makes them fat.
    (B) It makes them multiply.
    (C) It speeds up their lifecycle.
    (D) It slows down their lifecycle.

3. What does the professor mean when she says this: ⌒ ?

    (A) Everyone knows that exercise is good for you.
    (B) Many people have trouble exercising regularly.
    (C) It is surprising that more people don't exercise.
    (D) Both A and B

4. What is the professor's attitude toward smoking?

    (A) Unconcerned
    (B) Very negative
    (C) Indifferent
    (D) Positive

5. How is the lecture organized?

    (A) Cause and effect
    (B) Chronological order
    (C) By categories
    (D) Problems and solutions

6. What can be inferred about living a long life?

    (A) It is out of our control.
    (B) We can do many things to help us live longer.
    (C) How long we live is determined by our genes.
    (D) It is impossible to predict how long a person will live.

Listen to the lecture and take notes. **Track 3-33**

Steps in the spread of
the Brothers Grimm stories

- language

- popular

- translated

Step 1	Step 2	Step 3	Step 4	Step 5
	The brothers publish the stories			

Choose the correct answers. **Track 3-34**

1. What is the main topic of the lecture?

(A) The origin of fairy tales
(B) The spread of the Brothers Grimm fairy tales
(C) The Grimm Brothers' study of language
(D) Common fairy tales

2. According to the professor, what resulted from the Grimm Brothers' study of language?

(A) They learned new details about spoken language.
(B) They listened to peoples' life stories.
(C) They wrote down folk stories.
(D) They began to write fairy tales.

3. What does the professor imply when she says this: ( ) ?

   (A) That most books are not translated into other languages

   (B) That it was translated sooner after being published than most books

   (C) That it was translated later after being published than most books

   (D) That it is surprising that is was translated into English

4. What is the professor's attitude toward the Grimm Brothers' stories; when she says this: ( ) ?

   (A) She doesn't like them.

   (B) She is surprised they are so popular.

   (C) She likes them a lot.

   (D) She thinks the movies are better than the stories.

5. Why does the professor mention that the Grimm Brothers' studied language?

   (A) This was the brothers' job.

   (B) This is how the brothers heard the folk tales.

   (C) This is what the brothers are famous for.

   (D) This is what they did before they wrote fairy tales.

6. Which of the following is true according to the lecture? Place a checkmark in the correct box.

	True	False
(A) The Grimm Brothers' created the fairy tales.		
(B) The Grimm Brothers' studied language.		
(C) *Snow White* is one of Grimm's Fairy Tales.		
(D) *Cinderella* is not one of Grimm's Fairy Tales.		
(E) Grimm's Fairy Tales were translated into English less than ten years after being published.		

Listen to the lecture and take notes. **Track 3-35**

Red Cross's response to the floods in Mexico

- "family linking"

- supplies

- medical center

rain and no flood control ⟶

⟶ hospitals and schools closed, many homeless people

⟶

⟶

⟶

Choose the correct answers. **Track 3-36**

1. What is the lecture mainly about?

(A) Floods in Mexico
(B) The Red Cross response to floods in Mexico
(C) The Red Cross
(D) How to help people during a flood

2. According to the professor, what is one way that the Red Cross can help people who have lost their homes?

(A) Build new ones
(B) Give money to build new homes
(C) Evacuate people to safe areas
(D) Put people in hotels until their homes are safe

3. What does the professor mean when he says this: 🎧 ?

    (A) Mexico is not used to floods.

    (B) Mexico is used to floods, but this one was very bad.

    (C) Mexico has never had a flood before.

    (D) Mexico has had many floods, so this one wasn't bad.

4. What is the professor's opinion of the Red Cross?

    (A) Negative

    (B) Positive

    (C) Neutral

    (D) Loathing

5. Why does the professor mention medical centers?

    (A) To show some of the facilities that were damaged by the flood

    (B) To show how the Red Cross responded to hospitals being closed

    (C) To show how the Red Cross responded to homeless people

    (D) To show how the Red Cross responded to a lack of food

6. Which of the following is mentioned in the lecture about the Red Cross's response to the floods in Mexico? Place a checkmark in the correct box.

Statement	Yes	No
(A) The Red Cross built thousands of houses.		
(B) The Red Cross evacuated people to safer areas.		
(C) The Red Cross raised millions of dollars.		
(D) The Red Cross helped people find their family members.		
(E) The Red Cross setup medical centers.		

Conversation 2

🎧 Listen to the conversation and take notes. `Track 3-37`

Man - Student	Woman - Financial Assistance Officer
• Says he needs to speak to _____ _____ • Asks if he has come _____ _____ • Says he is a _____ _____ _____ _____ _____ _____	• Asks if he is a _____. If he is, he has _____ • They offer _____ to students, but _____ _____ • Asks how she can help • Says he might be eligible for _____ _____ _____ _____ _____

Choose the correct answers. `Track 3-38`

1. What is the conversation mainly about?

(A) The student needs some financial assistance.
(B) The student wants to loan a friend some money.
(C) The student is looking for a part-time job.
(D) The student wants to deposit some money in an account.

2. According to the woman, what type of loan is the student eligible for?

(A) An emergency student loan
(B) An annual income loan
(C) A part-time loan
(D) A genuine loan

3. Why does the student mention his apartment owner?

(A) Because he is applying for the loan for his apartment owner
(B) Because he owes his apartment owner money
(C) Because the woman knows his apartment owner
(D) Because he and his apartment owner are friends

4. What can be inferred about the student's apartment owner?

(A) He is happy that the student's rent is late.
(B) He is unhappy that the student's rent is late.
(C) He doesn't care that the student's rent is late.
(D) He owes the student money.

Basic Skills for the
TOEFL® iBT 3

Iain Donald Binns
Jonathan Wrigglesworth

Listening

Transcript & Answer Key

Transcripts

[Unit 1]

Conversation

Page 8

Practice

W: Excuse me, Professor Taylor, I was wondering if I could consult you about something?

M: Well, you can try. What would you like to know?

W: I have decided to change my degree. I wanted to ask you what subjects are incorporated in the Communication Degree. I always thought it sounded interesting, but I don't know much about it.

M: I see. Well first of all, are you sure that you want to change your degree? You will have to attend a bridging course first.

W: Yes, professor, I understand, but I'm really not enjoying the degree I am doing right now.

M: All right then, the communication courses look at areas such as advertising, public relations, and marketing. You will also study a lot of the theory behind these businesses. (*Practice A ends.*)

W: So these are the main parts of the degree then?

M: Well, these are some of them. You will also study many other aspects of the media. And of course, there is the ongoing training.

W: Oh really? That sounds interesting. What kind of work experience will I get?

M: Many different types of work experience are offered as part of the degree criteria.

W: Wow, that sounds really exciting. It sounds like a great degree.

M: Remember, though, that there is a lot of work involved, too. It is not all about getting the chance to work in the media. You have to do a lot of studying, too.

W: Yes, professor, I can see that. Thank you so much for your help. I have a much better idea of what I would like to do now.

M: You are welcome. I hope that you make the right decision in choosing a new degree.

Page 10

Test

M: Hello, professor. I was hoping that I might ask you a few questions about the graphic design class.

W: Certainly, William, are you thinking of signing up for it next term?

M: Yes, professor, I am considering it as one of my options right now. I have been looking at the public relations and marketing classes, too.

W: I see. What would you like to know about the graphic design class?

M: Well, mainly I would like to find out how the class is graded. What kinds of exams or assignments are involved in it?

W: OK, let me show you a copy of the class syllabus. As you can see in the course criteria, the assessments incorporate a mix of written work, some individual projects, and ongoing assessments of your work in class.

M: That sounds quite interesting. So there are no big exams at the end of the class.

W: No, William, the assessments are ongoing throughout the semester. There is no large exam at the end of the class.

M: That sounds wonderful. Is any kind of work experience offered in the class?

W: No, not in this class. The class is too short for students to be able to get real experience in the industry.

M: I see, it still sounds very interesting. I was also wondering if classroom attendance is taken into consideration.

W: Yes, of course it is. As with most other classes, you must attend at least forty percent of all classes.

M: Oh, right, of course.

W: So do you think that you would like to sign up for the class?

M: I would also like to consult the other professors about the marketing and public relations classes. May I get back to you tomorrow? Thank you for your help.

W: No problem, William, take care.

Page 12

Practice

M: Almost everything we use is made by machines. In the past, most things used to be made by hand. The Industrial Revolution was when things began to be made by machine. Does anyone know when and where the Industrial Revolution began?

W: I don't know when, but didn't it begin in Europe?

M: It began in the late 1800s in the textile industry in England. Slowly, large factories began to replace small workshops. People began to move off farms to cities to find work in factories. This was one of the largest migrations in human history. Three main factors led to the Industrial Revolution. These were the rule of law, an increased workforce, and improved transportation, specifically railroads and shipping. Let's discuss these. (*Practice A ends.*)

W: You said the rule of law. What does that mean?

M: The rule of law means that society is run by laws. Everyone must follow the law. This meant that property could not be taken without reason. Before the rule of law, the king and queen could take property. The rule of law restricted the power of the king and queen. To build new industries, people must be willing to invest in new ideas. The rule of law protected peoples' investments. People who invested in new ideas could make huge fortunes.

The Industrial Revolution needed more than just the rule of law. It needed people to work in the factories. Two things happened to increase the workforce. Fewer people had to work on farms because of better farming methods. Because of improved disease prevention, people were living longer. Because of these two factors, there was an available workforce.

Finally, raw materials had to be moved to the factories. Then goods had to be moved to customers. Better railroads and ships moved raw materials to factories. Finished products were exported to customers around the world.

Pages 14–15

Test

M: The Industrial Revolution changed the way things were made. It also changed society. What kinds of social changes do you think the Industrial Revolution made?

W: The first thing was that it created factories.

M: That's right. The Industrial Revolution created the first factories. It was important to be able to move raw materials to the factories and to be able to export goods overseas. Because of this, factories were built near transportation centers. Cities began to grow around these factories.

W: Is that why so many cities today are near rivers?

M: Yes, rivers were important for transportation. Cities also grew near railroads and sea ports. Of course many of these cities already existed. But they grew much larger as the factories grew. Some large cities grew near natural resources. Several cities grew near coal fields.

W: Cities had been around for a long time. What was different about these cities?

M: The first thing was the size. Cities in the industrial age were much bigger than previous cities. People lived close together in small apartments. The cities were dirty. There were many coal-burning factories. The coal polluted the air. Coal dust also collected on the ground.

W: This must have been a big change for people.

M: Yes, it changed the way people lived and worked. The majority of people had always lived in the countryside. Factories created a huge migration to the cities. By the end of the Industrial Revolution, the majority of the workforce lived in cities. Workers were no longer restricted to working on a farm. They could now search for higher wages in a factory job. But the working conditions were poor. A worker had to work hard or lose their job. And child labor became an issue. Factory owners wanted to hire people at the lowest wages possible. This meant hiring children. Children often had to work many hours. They also did difficult and dangerous work. Later, child labor was outlawed.

W: Was that the only social change?

M: No. The growth of cities and the migration of the workforce were major changes. But they weren't the only ones. Working in factories changed families. For the first time, most people were working outside of the home. This put a lot of stress on families. Sometimes, both parents worked in factories.

[Unit 2]

Conversation

Page 18

Practice

M: Excuse me, I'm trying to locate the school accommodation office. Is this it?

W: As a matter of fact, it is. How can I help you?

M: Oh wonderful, I would like to speak to someone about extending my stay in my student accommodation over the summer. Do you know if this is possible?

W: Yes, it is possible, but it really depends on your reason for extending your stay. May I have your name and student card so that I can look up your details? (*Practice A ends.*)

M: Sure, my name is Tom Andrews, and here is my card.

W: Thank you. Now I will just input your information into the computer. Ah, yes. I see that you have been staying in apartment 104 in the central building. Is that correct?

M: Yes, that is right.

W: Good, now that we have this established, may I ask why you would like to extend your stay over the summer vacation?

M: No problem. I will be going into my final year of my degree here at the school after the summer and would really like to keep the same room and apartment if possible. I have grown somewhat attached to it over the last year.

W: All right, I understand. They are very desirable apartments and a lot of students request them.

M: Yes, I am aware of that and would really like to stay there again next year.

W: It would also mean that you would not have to pay another deposit on the apartment. We would simply keep your initial deposit.

M: That would be great.

W: All right, Mr. Andrews, I will administrate this for you so that you can extend your stay over the summer and for the next school year.

M: Thank you very much. That is very kind of you. Goodbye.

Page 20

Test

W: Excuse me, I was wondering if you could help me.

M: Hello there, I will certainly do my best to help. What can I do for you?

W: My name is Maria Escobar, and I am an overseas student from Spain. I have decided to spend another semester here at the school. I would like to establish whether I could get student accommodation next semester.

M: I understand, Maria. May I see your student card so that I can input the information into my computer and find your details?

W: Certainly, here you are. I hope you can locate some.

M: Don't worry; here are a few. Now, would you like to keep the same accommodation, or would you mind changing apartments? It is actually somewhat easier to administrate a change of apartments. This is because many students like to keep the same apartment, and it takes time to organize their deposits for each year.

W: Oh really? That is fine. I do not mind moving into another apartment. As a matter of fact, I didn't like my last apartment very much. It was very small.

M: I see. Well, let me try to find something a little more desirable for you.

W: Thank you, that is very kind of you.

M: Yes, we have an opening in an apartment in the new student accommodation building. It is larger than your last place, but the deposit and rent are a little higher too.

W: OK. May I use the deposit from my initial apartment for this one?

M: Yes, that would be fine.

W: That's great, thank you. When would I be able to move into the apartment?

M: Anytime in the week before the next semester begins would be good.

W: That sounds perfect. Thank you again for your assistance.

Lecture

Page 22

Practice

W: How many of you enjoy going to the movies? As I thought—almost everyone. Most people enjoy the movies. People have enjoyed watching movies for over 100 years. All movies have some things in common. They all have a moving picture. And all movies tell a story. But movies have changed in the last 100 years. The so-called era of modern movies began with *Citizen Kane*.

Orson Welles wrote and directed *Citizen Kane*. He used new methods to make this movie. These new methods became widespread in later movies. Let's look at the similarities and differences between movies made before and after *Citizen Kane*. We will look at the type of photography used, the changes between scenes, and the make-up used. (*Practice A ends.*)

Citizen Kane introduced deep focus photography. This allows objects close and far to remain in focus. This is like a person's natural vision. Actors could now move around the set. Their interaction was more natural. This is common in today's movies. In earlier movies, only a narrow range could stay in focus. The actors couldn't move too much. Their interaction was unnatural. Welles also changed the way sound was used in movies. He linked sounds and phrases between scenes. This makes a smooth change between scenes. Movies used to use a blank screen and silence between scenes. Movies made before the 1940s often seem choppy. Modern movies have much more of a flow to them. We can thank Orson Welles for this.

Citizen Kane used special effects makeup. The story takes place over many years. The actors had to age with the progression of the story. Makeup artist Mel Berns was able to make the actors look almost any age. Makeup was nothing new to movies, but the techniques used by Berns were new. Special effects makeup is important to modern movies.

Pages 24–25

Test

W: Before I go on, has anyone heard about the radio program *War of the Worlds*? It was a show about an alien invasion.
M: Yes, I've heard of it. Didn't some people think it was real?
W: That's right. Actually, a lot of people thought it was really happening.
M: The people must have been a little stupid to have thought that.
W: I don't know about being stupid. We have already learned how Welles used new methods in the movie *Citizen Kane* to make it seem more real. Does anyone remember what methods he used?
M: He used deep focus photography, sound, and makeup.
W: Right. Obviously, a radio program doesn't use vision, so it wouldn't use photography or makeup. But both *Citizen Kane* and *War of the Worlds* used sound to make them seem more real. Let's take a look at the methods Welles used to create realism in a movie and a radio show.

The radio show was broadcast as if it were a news program. The news of a so-called alien invasion interrupted a music program. *War of the Worlds* broadcast alternated between news of the invasion and the music program. The interaction of these two programs added to the realism. Remember, in *Citizen Kane*, Welles also used changes between scenes to make the movie seem real.
M: That doesn't sound like a radio show.
W: That's exactly what Welles wanted. He went to great lengths to make the show sound like a newscast. He had the actors make mistakes, just as people do when they are talking naturally. This is unlike a movie like *Citizen Kane* where actors read from the script. The result was that the progression of the show was so realistic that thousands of people believed that the Earth was being invaded by aliens. There was widespread panic. People called the police. Thousands of people got into their cars and tried to leave the city.

In both *Citizen Kane* and *War of the Worlds*, Welles used crowd noises and voices to make it seem real. He had conversations recorded by actors running in the background, just as you might hear if you were in a crowd. In *War of the Worlds*, he also created realistic background sound effects.

One difference was the use of music. In *Citizen Kane*, Welles used music to highlight the character's moods. In *War of the Worlds*, there was no music during the newscasts, but music was used to fool people that there was a real music program playing.

[Unit 3]

Conversation

Pages 28–29

Practice

M: Excuse me, is this where the internship interviews are being held?

W: Yes, you came to the right place. It can be easy to get lost in a job convention this big. Can I have your name?

M: My name is Jackson Payne.

W: Thank you. Did you prearrange any interviews today?

M: Yes, in fact, I confirmed two interviews yesterday. Is there a problem?

W: No, I just want to make sure I let the correct supervisors know you are here. (*Practice A ends.*) Sometimes it can get confusing during a job convention. There are a lot of students interviewing.

M: Yeah, there are loads here. Do many students get internships at job conventions like this one?

W: Yes. I have seen quite a few students receive internship opportunities from conventions like this one.

M: Is it typical for most students to get an internship at the end of their junior year?

W: Yes. I would estimate that eighty-five percent of students get internships before their final year in college to determine if it is the job field they are interested in.

M: That is a good thing to know. Thank you. I should let you get back to your work. Is there somewhere I should wait for my interviews?

W: You can have a seat and wait right here. Also, would you mind filling out this form?

M: Sure, what's it for?

W: We want to see just who came to this convention and how we can make it better. It will help us with our research. You can check the box that says not to use your name if you want to remain anonymous.

M: OK, no problem.

W: Thank you very much. Good luck in your interviews.

Page 30

Test

W: Is this the career office?

M: Yes it is. Is there something I can help you with?

W: My advisor told me this is the place to come to for a job related to my major.

M: We definitely can help you do that here. I will need to ask you a few questions first, and then I will arrange a time for you to see a career counselor. Does that sound good?

W: Great.

M: OK, what is your name?

W: Samantha Kovach.

M: What is your field of study, and have you done an internship yet?

W: My major is architecture. I have had an internship the past two summers at an architecture firm downtown.

M: Are you graduating this spring?

W: Yes.

M: Do you have a preference as to where you want to work?

W: No . . . not really. I would like to stay in the city.

M: OK. That's all the questions I have for you. What time works best for you to come back in? We have an opening this afternoon.

W: I'll take it. I have nothing going on this afternoon. Can I ask you a question?

M: Sure. I'll do my best to answer.

W: Do many students get jobs through the career center?

M: I'm going to estimate about seventy percent of students who come in get jobs. It is definitely going to be to your advantage that you have had internships before. Also, since the university has such a great architecture program, job placement has been good.

W: That's encouraging to hear. What time do I need to be here this afternoon?

M: Your appointment is at three o'clock. You should show up fifteen minutes before in case there is anything for you to fill out.

W: Great. Thanks for your help, and I'll see you this afternoon.

M: See you later.

Transcripts

Pages 32–33

Practice

M: Can anyone tell us what a genome is?

W: I'm not sure exactly what it is, but I think it has to do with genes.

M: Yes, you're on the right track. A genome is a map of the genes and chromosomes in a living organism. This science is only a few decades old. But it could solve many problems.

Genomic research is mapping genes. It is also creating helpful new organisms. This is done by the manipulation of genes. This will be useful in medicine. It has many more uses. We are all concerned about the problems of fuel use and pollution. Let me highlight a few of the ways genome science offers possible solutions for making fuels, cleaning pollution, and warning of pollution. (*Practice A ends.*)

The world is running out of energy. Genomic science could help to make bio-fuels. Bacteria are usually thought of as being bad. But bacteria may be used to produce energy. Bacteria could make an efficient fuel.

Pollution is another pressing problem. We may be able to create bacteria that eat pollution. These bacteria will only eat a desired pollutant. These bacteria could be released into a polluted area. They would dispose of the pollution. Then people would collect them. Or some bacteria might do their job and die.

Bacteria could also be used as a warning device. Bacteria could be made to detect dangerous toxins. This mechanism would give us an early warning. This could help us make changes before they become a large problem.

This is an exciting area of research. There are many ways that DNA research will help us. Medicine is probably the area with the most potential. We will talk about that in the next lecture.

Pages 34–35

Test

M: Some of you have asked me to talk about why genome research is so important to medicine. DNA research has the potential to find cures or treatment for almost every disease by manipulation of bits of DNA.

W: What do you mean by manipulation?

M: A genome tells us exactly what the DNA sequence is. Once we know what bit of DNA causes a disease, it will soon be possible to turn that DNA bit off or on.

W: Doesn't that mean DNA research is only useful for genetic diseases?

M: No. Every disease begins in one of three ways. A DNA sequence in the body can cause some diseases. The DNA in bacteria causes some diseases. And DNA in viruses causes some diseases. DNA research has the potential to dispose of all diseases.

W: So all diseases can be cured once we know what DNA causes the disease. And once we know how to turn the DNA bit on and off.

M: That's right. This is a very exciting field of research.

W: Can you give us an example of how this mechanism would work?

M: Yes, let's look at cancer to highlight how the mechanism would work. Many types of cancer are the result of a person's DNA. Once we have discovered what bit of DNA causes a cancer, we can run tests to detect if a person has that DNA sequence. If a person has the cancer-causing DNA, we can begin to treat it. The treatment would turn that bit of DNA off.

W: So does that mean people could be treated to prevent cancer?

M: Right. You wouldn't have to wait until you got the disease. You could be treated and not have to worry about it.

W: So I could be tested for all types of cancer now, and I wouldn't have to worry about ever getting cancer.

M: You could still do things that might cause cancer, such as smoke cigarettes. But you are right. It will be possible to be tested for cancer-causing DNA, and then be treated, so your risk of getting cancer would be very low.

W: You mentioned earlier that diseases are also caused by bacteria and viruses. How would DNA help cure these types of diseases?

M: For example, if you were exposed to a virus, the treatment would turn the DNA in the virus off, and it would die. This would be the same approach with bacteria.

[Unit 4]

Conversation

Page 38

Practice

W: Hello, Professor Davis! Do you have a minute to answer a few questions on the semester assignment?

M: Sure, Katherine. . . come in and take a seat. What questions do you have?

W: I'm working on interviewing people for the project, and I need some advice. This is my first time doing an assignment like this. Do you think you can give me a few tips on how to interview? (*Practice A ends.*)

M: It can be intimidating, especially if it is your first time. It is important to have a good attitude when you interview people. They are not going to want to talk to you if you are not interested in the task you are doing. Also, make sure people understand the questions you are asking them.

W: What do you mean?

M: It might help if you went prepared with a survey for your participants to fill out. Surveys are a great way to gather information about a subject from a lot of people. They help people understand what information you need to know. Before you start interviewing, make sure you are given consent to use the information they share with you.

W: This task sounds intense.

M: It is not an easy task, but once you do it, it isn't so intense.

W: Is there anything else I should know?

M: The other important thing is to have good comprehension of what you are surveying people about. People will ask you questions, and you want to be able to answer their questions.

W: I am confident in my comprehension of the subject, but I am nervous about asking random people questions.

M: I think you will do fine.

W: Thanks, Professor Davis.

M: You're welcome, Katherine, and let me know if you run into any problems.

Page 40

Test

M: Janet, you seem nervous about the assignment I handed out in class today. Are you going to have a hard time gathering information for this project?

W: Professor Chambers, I have to admit I am not looking forward to doing this project. It is a bit intense for me. I have no problem gathering information, but I am not very good at interviewing people. It is intimidating to ask questions to people I don't know.

M: I understand Janet. I don't know too many students who like to interview strangers. For most students, the more practice you get at interviewing, the easier it gets.

W: I'm not sure interviewing people I don't know is ever going to be easy for me.

M: You will do fine. Just make sure you have good comprehension of the material. It helps to have a good attitude, too.

W: You make it sound so easy. Is there any other option I have to complete this assignment? Can I mail surveys to people?

M: I'm sorry, Janet, there is no other option. If you want to mail surveys to people that is fine with me. You will still need to interview at least ten people.

W: Why are you having us interview people?

M: Since this is a class about communication styles, I want you to learn how to communicate with people you don't know.

W: What if I can't find anyone to interview?

M: If you cannot find people to interview let me know, and I might be able to help you.

W: When does this project need to be done?

M: You have until the end of the semester. That means you have about two months. I think that should be plenty of time for you to interview ten people.

W: Thanks, Professor Chambers, for answering all my questions.

M: You're welcome, and come back to my office if you think of more.

Transcripts

Pages 42–43

Practice

W: Lifting or moving objects is only one thing muscles do. Muscles have several uses. We use our muscles to move our bodies and to move other objects. Muscles are also used to produce heat and to keep many parts of our bodies working. There are three types of muscles: skeletal, heart, and smooth. (*Practice A ends.*)

Skeletal muscle is what most of us think of when we think of muscle. These are the muscles we use to move our bodies and to move other objects. They are named for their location. As the name implies, they are attached to bones. These muscles are striped with alternating light and dark bands. We can move these muscles by thinking. This makes them different from other types of muscles. Skeletal muscles can be divided into "fast twitch" and "slow twitch" muscles. "Fast twitch" muscles are used to move quickly for a short distance. They must also rest for a short interval before being used again. People who run short distances quickly have a lot of fast twitch muscles. Slow twitch muscles are used to move over long distances. It is these muscles that are used by long distance runners.

The heart muscle is only found in the heart. Nevertheless, it is the most important type of muscle. This type of muscle forms the bulk of the wall of the heart. Like the skeletal muscle, the heart muscle is striped with light and dark bands. Unlike the skeletal muscle, the heart muscle cannot be moved by thinking.

The final type of muscle is smooth muscle. This type of muscle is found in the hollow internal structures of the body, such as blood vessels and the stomach. Unlike skeletal and heart muscles, smooth muscles are not striped. Like heart muscles, they cannot be moved by thinking.

Pages 44–45

Test

W: Last week, we learned about the different types of muscles. Does anyone remember what they are?
M: Yes, I think they are skeletal muscles, heart muscles, and smooth muscles.
W: That's right. Muscles are named for how they look and their location. For example smooth muscles are non-striped, skeletal muscles are attached to bones, and the heart muscle is located in the heart with alternating light and dark bands.

Today, we will continue our discussion of the human body. We will discuss bones. There are 206 bones in the human body. Don't worry; you don't need to learn them all. Bones can be grouped into types: we will be learning the types of bones. We all know that bones make up our skeleton, but not all bones are the same. There are five types of bones that are classified by their shape and size. Different types of bones also have different functions.

Although bones are internal, we all have an idea of what a bone looks like. What do you think of when you think of a bone?
M: I think of something like a leg bone—long, hard, and thin.
W: That is what most of us think of when we talk about bones, something long and thin. These are called "long" bones. As the name implies, they are longer than they are wide. Leg bones and arm bones are types of long bones. Long bones are the hardest type of bone. Nevertheless, they are the most likely to break.

In addition to long bones, we also have short bones. Short bones are almost as wide as they are long. They are shaped similar to a cube. Examples of short bones are the bones in our fingers and toes.

The next group of bones is used for protection; they are called "flat" bones. Can anyone think of an example of a flat bone?
M: How about the skull?
W: Yes, the bones that make up our skulls are probably the best examples of flat bones. Another type of bones is the "irregular" bones. These bones come in different shapes depending on their function. The bones that make up our backbone are a good example of irregular bones. They are placed at regular intervals, but each has a unique shape.

The last type of bones is the "round" bones. An example of a round bone is the knee cap. These bones help joints to move.

[Unit 5]

Page 48
Practice

W: Good afternoon. Welcome to the career office. How may I help you?

M: Hi, my name is Brian Jones. I have an appointment to meet with a career counselor.

W: Of course. Hello Brian. Please have a seat. What would you like to talk about today?

M: Well, I am going to graduate from the cooking program at the end of the semester, and I was looking for a little advice on what I should do afterward. (*Practice A ends.*)

W: All right Brian, I assume that you would like to work in the catering business once you have graduated?

M: Yes, I would like to be a chef in the future.

W: That is great. I can see that you are passionate about cooking. That will be very helpful to you in finding a job.

M: That is good to know. I would really like to find employment in a restaurant if that is possible.

W: OK, I will see if we can find you some face-to-face interviews. I think that it would be beneficial to start looking for work as soon as possible. Now let me take a few notes to pass on to potential employers. How would you categorize your skills in the workplace?

M: Well, let me see. I am hard working, honest, disciplined, and I work well under pressure.

W: That is excellent. Those are important qualities to have in the catering profession.

M: Also, in my studies I specialized in making desserts and pastries. I guess that it is one of my main strengths.

W: How lovely! We should not have too much trouble in finding you a placement or position as a pastry chef. I will start contacting some businesses for you, and I will get in touch with you soon.

M: That is fantastic. Thank you so much for your help. I look forward to hearing from you in the future.

Page 50
Test

W: Hello, sorry to bother you. I was hoping that you could help me.

M: Hi, sure. Do you have an appointment?

W: Oh, I'm sorry I don't. I was just passing by and realized that you may be able to help me find a work placement for the summer.

M: I see, well that is something that we specialize in here at the career office. You should really have made an appointment, though.

W: Sorry. Can I make one now?

M: Actually, we are not too busy right now, so don't worry about it this time.

W: Wow, thank you so much. I really appreciate this.

M: That's OK. Now may I have some information?

W: Sure! I'm a first year student studying biology. And I would like to find a placement that would give me some experience over the summer if possible.

M: OK, that may be a little difficult as there are not too many jobs available in biology, but we will do our best for you. Now, do you have any prior experience in the workplace?

W: Not really. Before I became a student, I worked in catering for three months but that has been my only job so far.

M: That's OK. You sound like you are quite passionate about biology, and face-to-face you seem like a nice person. As long as you are disciplined, then you should do well.

W: Oh, thanks. I was a little worried about my lack of experience.

M: Don't worry; I wouldn't categorize that as a huge problem. Everyone has to start somewhere. I will keep an eye out for you and get in touch with you if any placements become available.

W: That is great, thank you.

M: You are welcome, and any other time that you need career advice before you graduate or even afterward, this office is here to help you. Goodbye.

Page 52
Practice

W: It is surprising how many people are ignorant about the stock market. The term stock market historically refers to a public place where things are bought and sold. Since before our economy was industrialized, it has meant the buying and selling of shares in businesses.

Now that we know what a stock market is, why do people trade stocks?

M: Well, I trade stocks because I want to get rich.

W: Exactly! We trade stocks to make money. Today, we are going to go over three steps you need to know to successfully trade stocks—decide on your goals, then assess the market, and then get a stock broker. (*Practice A ends.*)

The first thing you need to do if you want to trade stocks is to decide on your goals. Of course, everyone who trades stocks wants to make money. So that part of your goal is obvious. You need to decide how you want to make money. Do you want to take a chance and maybe make money quickly or lose money quickly? Or do you want to play it safe and try to make (or lose) a smaller amount of money over a long time. Once you have decided which is best for you, you can move on to the next step.

Now it is time to assess the stock market. Learn about different industries and companies. See if you can find a couple of industries that you think might do well over the next few years, and then find the best companies in those industries. Now, you "pencil" trade. Take a month and pretend that you have bought some stocks. Pretend to buy and sell and chart how you do. Once you feel comfortable with how your stocks are doing, it is time to move on to the next step.

Finally, you find a stock broker. Try to find a broker who you feel comfortable with and who will give you advice. Once you have done this, it is time to buy some stocks.

Pages 54–55

Test

W: Last week, we talked about steps to buying stocks. Many people are ignorant of the risks of buying stocks. To make sure that you understand that it is possible to lose money in the stock market, we are going to talk about the steps that led to the Great Depression. Historically, this was the worst economic depression in American history.

M: It seems like the stock market is always going up. I thought that stocks were safe.

W: The stock market usually does go up. And stocks are usually safe, but everything has risks. Before you buy stocks, you should assess the industry in which you want to invest.

Let's look at the five steps that led to the Great Depression so you can see what can go wrong with stocks. An economic depression is a period of little or no growth in the economy. During a depression, there are usually fewer jobs, and people have difficulty earning money.

The beginning of the Great Depression was on "Black Tuesday," October 29, 1929. On this date, the price of stocks dropped suddenly. This is often called "The Crash." This drop was huge. No one had seen anything like it before.

M: If the price of stock went down, wouldn't that be good if you wanted to buy?

W: Well, no. The prices fell so fast that no one wanted to buy. Stocks became almost worthless. The next step was bank failures. Banks began to fail and close. Many people lost all of their money.

Next was a drop in buying. Because so many people had lost money in the stock market crash and bank failures, they didn't have money to buy anything except food. No one was buying things. And because people weren't buying, companies weren't selling as much. This meant that people reduced their manufacturing, so there were fewer jobs. This was especially true in the industrialized Northeast, where factories closed.

Then economic policies also added to the depression. The government tried to protect US businesses. This led to less trade with other countries. American companies had no one to sell their products to. This deepened the depression.

The last condition that led to the Great Depression was the drought of 1930. A severe drought hit the Great Plains part of America. Farmers couldn't grow crops. Many farmers couldn't pay their bills and lost their farms.

The country went through nearly ten years of hard economic times. It wasn't until World War II that the country finally came out of the Great Depression.

[Unit 6]

Conversation

Page 58

Practice

M: Hi, could I order the usual cheeseburger with French fries and coleslaw on the side please? I don't see it on the menu today like it normally is. Why is that?

W: Actually sir, I'm afraid that the school canteen will not be serving that kind of junk food anymore. Can I offer you some pasta salad or perhaps some quiche?

M: What? Why? Why can't you give me a cheeseburger any more? I have been eating them here at the cafeteria for the last two years. Nobody wants to eat pasta or quiche every day. This just isn't rational. (*Practice A ends.*)

W: I'm sorry sir, but the school board has decided, on our behalf, that we can no longer advocate an unhealthy diet for students. So we had to change the menu plan, I'm afraid.

M: Really? Well I am an active and healthy student, and I exercise regularly. I certainly don't have a problem with my health or obesity. The idea that the school board can decide what I may or may not eat is stupid. That concept seems very outdated to me.

W: I understand how you feel, sir. I think they have overreacted about the lack of nutrition in young adults' diets. It's sad, but I'm afraid there is nothing we can do about it. Changes to the type of food that the cafeteria serves are at the school board's discretion.

M: I am not happy to hear the changes made were involuntary. You made wonderful cheeseburgers. I don't know what I will do for my lunch now.

W: I know you may feel the reasons for the change in the menu plan are a little arbitrary, but you should give the new healthy menu a try. There are a lot of nice new dishes on it.

M: All right, I will give it a go. Thank you for explaining everything.

W: You're welcome.

Page 60

Test

M: Hi, what can I get for you?

W: Oh, good afternoon. I'd like to order my lunch. Can you recommend something to me?

M: Sure. Have you been here before?

W: Actually no, I'm quite new here, and my friends usually order on my behalf. They know what is good. What do you think is best?

M: Well, actually, the lasagna with French fries is lovely. Would you like that?

W: I do like lasagna, but I am trying to avoid French fries and other junk food. I worry about nutrition sometimes. And obesity is becoming a big problem with people of my age these days. Could I have the lasagna with a salad instead?

M: Oh, I'm sorry, but the lasagna only comes as a dish with French fries.

W: But I would like a salad with it. Is that not possible? Can't you serve anything at your discretion?

M: I'm sorry, I know that seems as though it would be perfectly rational, but it is the policy of the cafeteria only to serve set dishes so as not to complicate things.

W: I see. Well that sounds like a bit of an outdated policy to me. Customers should be able to order what they want.

M: I understand what you are saying, but the decision is not arbitrary. In a small business like this school cafeteria, it is much easier to monitor what we are serving and what needs to be ordered if it is done this way.

W: I guess I can understand that. The options that you have must be limited in such a small place. I suppose I'll take the dish with French fries.

M: That's great. Here you are. I know your decision to eat the fries is involuntary, so I will give you a little salad on the side, too. Just this time, though.

W: Oh, thank you so much. Bye.

Page 62

Practice

W: American culture has a large influence around the world. American pop culture has never been more dominant. Young people all over the world wear Michael Jordan jerseys. Many people listen to Madonna songs. People all over the world watch American TV shows. Last year, eighty-eight of the top 100 movies in the world were American. What does all of this US culture do to other countries? Well, there is imitation of US styles, more racial understanding, and, unfortunately, exposure to poor quality entertainment and negative images of Americans. (*Practice A ends.*)

One result of American pop culture overseas is imitation. American pop music, television, movies, and street fashion have become popular around the world. Many countries have developed their own versions of US pop culture. Performers in Tokyo might dance with the same moves they see on a Britney Spears video. Or a Korean movie might be made in the same style as a Hollywood thriller. This may mean that some countries lose their own style of pop culture.

American pop culture has a lot of ethnic diversity. The world is full of racial discrimination and bias. American entertainers of all races are accepted around the world. Oprah Winfrey, an African American, is now one of the best known people in the world. This helps make people more understanding of other cultures.

Many of the TV shows and movies seen overseas are poor quality. Better quality television programs are more expensive. In many countries, only the poor quality American programs are seen. This may cause them to have a poor opinion of American entertainment.

In movies and TV, Americans are often seen doing negative things. Often the movies are violent or involve crimes. Viewers may never encounter an American. The movies may be the only information that many people get about America. Many people therefore think that Americans are violent or dishonest.

Pages 64–65

Test

W: Last week we talked about how dominant American entertainment is around the world. There were four effects that we mentioned. Does anyone remember what they are?
M: You talked about ethnic diversity. This can help fight racial discrimination and bias in the world. You also talked about how American entertainment is ethnically diverse, and that this is a good thing for people around the world to see. You also mentioned the poor quality of a lot of the US TV shows and movies that are seen overseas.
W: Yes, those are two of the four. Does anyone remember the other two?
M: You also mentioned the negative image that some American entertainment gives of Americans, and that other countries imitate American entertainment.
W: Yes, that is all four. Today, we are going to talk about a case of imitation. In this case, many people think the copy became better than the original. I'm talking about breakdancing. Breakdancing began in New York City and spread all over the world. It became so popular in one country that the best breakdancers now come from there and not America. Does anyone know what country I'm talking about?
M: I think it is South Korea. I've seen some Korean breakdancers on TV. They are very good.
W: That's right. South Korea has taken American breakdancing and made it better. This is an interesting example of imitation. Let's take a look at what caused breakdancing to become popular around the world.

Breakdancing began as street dancing. Some famous singers put it into their music videos. These music videos were seen all over the world. Many people fell in love with breakdancing. Breakdancing became a popular form of entertainment in many countries. But Korea embraced it like no other country. We can see that people watching breakdancing in music videos caused the popularity of breakdancing to grow in Korea. Now that Korea is known for having the best breakdancers in the world, is that affecting America?

Korea has several stage companies that put on dance shows and musicals. The Korean tourism board has dance competitions that bring dancers from all over the world. Korea is truly the center for breakdancing.

What is interesting is that breakdancing is less popular in America now. You rarely encounter breakdancing in America anymore. It is really the popularity of breakdancing in Korea that is keeping this art form alive.

M: So, breakdancing in American music videos caused this style of dance to become popular in Korea. Now the popularity of breakdancing in Korea is keeping the dance style alive.
W: Exactly.

[Review 1]

Conversation 1

Page 67

M: (*Knocking*) Hello, Professor Jones.
W: Hello, Matthew. I haven't seen you for a while. Come in and take a seat.
M: Thank you.
W: You haven't attended class for the last couple of weeks. Is everything OK?
M: My grandmother died, so I went home to spend time with my family. Initially, I planned to stay a week. Then I got sick while I was there, so I stayed there for a second week. I came by to see if I had missed a lot of work.
W: I'm sorry to hear about your grandmother. Actually, you have missed a lot. Last week, we reviewed the material for the mid-semester exam. I like to consult with my classes before I confirm what will be on an exam. In this case, I even let your class have some input into the content of the exam. Did you have time to study while you were at home?
M: Not really. I didn't take many books with me because I didn't know I'd be gone so long.
W: I see. Well, in order to graduate on time, it is a criterion that you pass this course. I hope you are feeling better and are ready to work now.
M: Yes, I'm feeling much better. Do you have any handouts that might help me?
W: I do. Here is the handout from last week's class. You will see that I've highlighted some of the more important areas. I estimate that you've got about ten hours of study ahead of you.
M: No problem. I told my boss that I had exams and wasn't available to work this week. I plan to focus my time this week on studying.
W: That's good to hear.
M: Well, thank you for taking this time to talk to me face-to-face.
W: It's my pleasure. Good luck with your studies and see you in class.

Lecture 1

Pages 68–69

M: Last week we talked about the art of the eighteenth century. Today we will talk about the progression of art movements. Can anyone tell me the next art movement?
W: Was it modern art?
M: Yes, that's correct. In the early twentieth century, four art movements were dominant. This can be seen as the beginning of modern art. These movements incorporated features of earlier artists, but they each brought original ideas to the art of the time. This period lasted only about ten years. The interaction of the old and new made for some interesting art.

Fauvism used intense colors and wild brush strokes. These paintings have beautiful colors. Gustave Moreau was a teacher of many of the Fauvists. He had a huge impact on these artists. He had an open mind. He taught his students to think for themselves. Matisse said, "He did not set us on the right roads, but off the roads." The leader of the Fauvists was Henri Matisse. The movement lasted only three years from 1905 to 1907. However, it had a lasting impact on other movements.

W: Were the Cubists around then?
M: Yes. Cubism is the most well known of these four movements. And Picasso is its best known artist. Cubists painted bits of the picture. They then put the bits together out of place. These art pieces appeared shocking to many people. African and Native American art influenced the cubists. These art forms were exported to Europe around this time. They quickly inspired artists there. The Cubists inspired works in music and literature. Cubism is still an influential art movement.

Expressionism distorts reality to show feelings. These paintings don't look like reality. But you still know what is being painted. Colors may be unnatural. Shapes may be exaggerated. But a person still looks like a person. A group of artists never called themselves Expressionists. This term was only used years later. Expressionism also influenced other media. It is still an active movement.

Transcripts

Futurism began in Italy. And the Russians quickly joined in. The Futurists wanted to rebel. They sought to be original. Much of their work was violent and chaotic. A sense of energy is often present. Patriotism separated the Futurists from other artists. They sought to glorify war, violence, and patriotism. The violence of WWI brought the movement to an end.

These artists inspired later generations. Their work is still displayed, and their influence can be seen all over the world.

Lecture 2

Pages 70–71

W: Today we are going to look at the two biggest makers of movies in the world. These are Hollywood and Bollywood. We all know about Hollywood. It's a city near Los Angeles. Historically, great movies have been made there. Bollywood isn't as well known. Does anyone know where Bollywood is?

M: It's in India. Many Indian movies are made there.

W: That's right. Bollywood is the nickname of the Indian movie industry. These movies are not well known in America. Nevertheless, they have widespread appeal all over the world. I said we were going to talk about the two biggest makers of movies in the world. Where are the most movies made each year?

M: All of the movies I see are made in Hollywood. So I'd say Hollywood.

W: Most people would agree with you. But they would be wrong. More movies are made in Bollywood than anywhere else in the world. This is somewhat surprising to many people. But Bollywood makes double the number of movies each year as Hollywood.

M: I have never seen a Bollywood movie. What are they like?

W: There are many differences between Bollywood and Hollywood movies. Most Bollywood movies are musicals. They have elaborate dance and musical numbers. This is uncommon in modern Hollywood movies.

Another difference is the length. The average Bollywood movie lasts three to four hours. The average Hollywood movie runs about two hours.

M: Four hours is a long movie. How do people sit that long?

W: Bollywood movies are mostly musicals. They have a lot of energy. They are fast paced. So, the time passes quickly. Afterward, you will want to see more.

In Bollywood, an actor might work on ten movies at the same time. In Hollywood, they usually work on only one at a time.

The majority of movies in Bollywood are romances. In Hollywood, there is a wider variety of themes.

They both spend huge amounts of money to promote their movies and stars. Hollywood already has a huge worldwide audience. Bollywood's worldwide exposure is growing. Several Bollywood movies have done well in the US, and Indian movies are common in British theaters.

Some people even think that Bollywood is beginning to influence Hollywood. In recent years, there have been several Hollywood musicals. This may be due to the widespread success of Bollywood musicals.

Lecture 3

Pages 72–73

W: In the last two weeks, we have talked about organisms and their lifecycles. Life cycles are only one type of cycle. In nature, most events are part of a larger cycle. Today, we are going to talk about one of the largest and most important cycles in nature, the water cycle. The water cycle is also called the hydrologic cycle. This involves the movement of water. Water naturally exists in three forms: ice, liquid, and gas. Every drop of water on Earth moves through these forms and through the water cycle. But the water cycle is being disrupted by human activity.

M: The water cycle—is that water changing from ice to liquid and to gas?

W: Well, that's part of it, but that's not the whole picture. Imagine a drop of water in the ocean. This drop of water enters the atmosphere by evaporation. As a gas, the drop of water floats in the air. It may join with other drops of water and form clouds. These clouds may float over land where the drop of water falls back to Earth as rain. On Earth, the drop of water might join a river or lake, become part of the groundwater, or fall back into the ocean. Every drop of water that falls will evaporate again. This is the water cycle. A drop of water usually spends nine days in the water cycle. But water in a glacier might stay there for 65,000 years.

M: You said the water cycle is important. Why is it important to us? I just turn on the water and there it is.

W: We all know that life on Earth wouldn't exist without water. And as people, we need fresh water. The demand for fresh water is growing every year, and the available supply of fresh water is shrinking. Already twenty-six countries are considered to be fresh water scarce. It is estimated that by 2025 we will have lost one-third of the world's fresh water.

M: Why are we losing our fresh water?

W: Increased use is part of the problem. But we also deplete the fresh water supply by wasting water and by clearing vegetation. A lack of vegetation and over building causes fresh water to run to the ocean quicker and become saltwater.

M: What can we do?

W: We can all be careful not to waste water. We can also protect against water runoff by protecting plants and green spaces.

Conversation 2

Page 74

W: Excuse me. Who should I speak to about finding a journal article?

M: Have you looked on the computer?

W: Yes, the computer says it should be in row L. But I can't see it.

M: OK. Let's look together. . . you're right. It's not there. Is Ethnic Studies something you're passionate about? This seems quite important to you.

W: Not really, but it is important for my course. I need to get a good grade in this course, as I want to do an internship next semester, and they will look at this grade. This assignment is worth fifty percent of my assessment for that class, so I need to do well. What should I do? Can I order one from somewhere else?

M: Sure. We can order one from another library. They usually arrive within a few days, but they can take up to a week to come. When do you need it by?

W: My assignment is due in four days, so I really need it today or tomorrow.

M: Oh, well I don't think that's going to be possible. Like I said, they take a few days at the earliest to arrive. And as tomorrow is Friday, they are unlikely to arrive until Monday. Is that when your paper is due?

W: Yes. It's due at five o'clock on Monday. What am I going to do?

M: Well, I could call around and see if a library nearby has one and get them to express it to us, but that will cost you some money. A regular order is free, but if we put a rush on the order, you'll have to pay for the express postage.

W: That's OK. I'm desperate, so I will pay anything.

M: OK, well I'll get on the phone and start calling around. I need you to sign here, to say that I have your consent to get it sent express postage.

W: Thank you for all your help. I'll come back afterward to see what you have found.

[Unit 7]

Conversation

Pages 76–77

Practice

M: Excuse me. Are you Lisa Jones?

W: Yes, that's me.

M: My name is Todd Phillips. I'm an employee of the university. I'm in charge of checking the dormitories to make sure they have working smoke detectors in them. Do you mind if I look in your room?

W: Um, actually. . .

M: If you have to go to class or something, I can let myself in. I have a master key to all the rooms in this dorm.

W: No, I'm not in a hurry. One moment, I'll open the door.

M: Thanks. This won't take long, I'm sure. (*Practice A ends.*) Uh-oh. I see a smoke detector up there, but the light is off. The battery probably burned out.

W: Excuse me, what are you doing with that chair?

M: I carry extra batteries with me. I'm just going to replace the battery in your smoke detector. Well, look at that. It doesn't have any batteries in it.

W: Actually, I removed the battery when I moved in.

M: Why did you do that?

W: Sometimes I smoke in here, like when the weather is bad or when it's really cold outside. I didn't want the smoke detector going off then.

M: You know the dorm policy is explicit when it forbids smoking in the dorms. It's incredibly dangerous. Not to mention that smoking makes the rooms smell bad for future residents.

W: I am aware of that, but I'm incredibly careful. And I just didn't want to go outside when it was cold.

M: Culprits caught smoking can be expelled from the dorm. You had better cut that out. I'm going to put a new battery in here, and I'm not going to mention your smoking to anyone because you have been genuine and honest about your indiscretion. Just don't do it anymore. If you want to smoke, please go outside.

W: Yeah, OK.

Page 78

Test

W: Excuse me. Are you Joe Park?

M: Yes, that's me.

W: My name is Elizabeth Jordan. I'm the dorm advisor in charge of these dormitories and the women's dormitories next door.

M: Uh. Hi. How can I be of assistance to you?

W: Well, there have been complaints about residents cooking food in their dorm rooms, and your name was listed as one of the culprits.

M: What's a culprit? Forgive me, my English isn't that great.

W: Oh, it's a person who has committed a crime.

M: A crime!

W: Uh, not a crime in this case. I hope that it is merely an indiscretion on your part. Would you mind if I looked in your room?

M: Um, actually. . .

W: If you are required to go to class or somewhere else, I can let myself in. I have a master key to all the rooms in this dormitory and the women's dormitories.

M: No, it's all right. Let me open the door.

W: Thanks. This won't take long. I see that you have a saucepan on your desk. And it has food in it.

M: Uh, yeah. I forgot to clean it before I went to class this morning.

W: Leaving dirty pots around the room attracts bugs and potentially even rats.

M: I was going to clean the pot after class.

W: That doesn't matter. In the dorm contract, it explicitly forbids residents from cooking in their rooms. There is the danger of starting a fire, even with the smoke detectors. I am being completely genuine about this. There is also the fact that the other residents in this dorm don't like the smell.

M: But the food in the cafeteria is incredibly bad. . .

W: You must obey the rules of this dormitory, Mr. Park. Consider this a warning. If I see any more evidence that you're cooking in your room, I will have you evicted from the dormitory. Is that understood?

M: Yes, Ms. Jordan.

Lecture

Pages 80

Practice

W: So you all know that William Shakespeare wrote a lot of famous plays. Maybe you saw some of the movies that were made from his plays. Has anyone seen the movie *Hamlet*? Or *Romeo and Juliet*? Some of you. Great! OK, well, I'm glad most of you are familiar with Shakespeare. But we're not going to talk about his plays. We're going to talk about his poems, his sonnets. Shakespeare wrote over 150 sonnets! You can find a listing of the first lines of all of Shakespeare's sonnets in the appendix of your text.

Now don't worry. We're not going to read all of the sonnets, only three of them. Why did I choose just three? Well, basically it is because Shakespeare's sonnets can be classified into three types—The Fair Youth, The Dark Lady, and Others. (*Practice A ends.*)

He wrote a lot of sonnets about a young man. This young man was very good looking— very handsome. Long ago, pretty or handsome people were called "fair," so in the poems, Shakespeare calls this character "Fair Youth." In all, 126 of Shakespeare's 154 sonnets were written to this fair youth! The sonnets are written like letters to this character.

Another character that Shakespeare wrote a lot of sonnets to was his "dark lady." It might sound bad because he called her dark. But this lady was someone that the poet loved. This is a contradiction that is difficult to explain. It may be that "dark" only refers to her aesthetics. Or it may refer to something about her personality. It is difficult for us to make a coherent argument either way. Shakespeare wrote twenty-six sonnets to the dark lady.

Finally, there was the third group of sonnets. Those are classified as sonnets about other things. Shakespeare wrote those sonnets about things that he thought were wrong with the world around him. Or he wrote about his own ideas, not to or about any character. There are two sonnets classified in this last category.

For clarity, let me say it again. We will be reading one sonnet from each of these groups.

Pages 82–83

Test

M: Last week we talked about Shakespeare's sonnets. Does anyone remember how his sonnets are usually classified?

W: I remember that he wrote to two characters. One was a dark lady. He also wrote to a fair youth.

M: That's right he wrote to a young man. He called the young man the fair youth. He also wrote to a woman he called the dark lady. There is also a third group of sonnets about things Shakespeare thought were wrong with the world. OK, so that was what we learned about his sonnets. Now, most of you have heard of Shakespeare because of his plays. Today we are going to look at how Shakespeare's plays are classified.

Shakespeare's plays are considered the greatest in the English language. But how do you think we can organize Shakespeare's plays into coherent groups like his sonnets are organized? Well, his plays can be divided into histories, comedies, and tragedies. He wrote in all three styles well. What an incredible writer he was!

Early in his career, Shakespeare wrote mostly histories. These were based on actual history and other writers' works. It seems strange to us today, but that was the aesthetics of the day. Audiences expected histories to be based on earlier works. Shakespeare's plays were written as if they were long poems. The poetry in his histories is simple. It wasn't until years later that his poetry became more complex. Today, the histories are known for the clarity of the writing and the power of the stories. Two of the more famous histories are *Richard III* and *Henry V*.

The next grouping is the comedies. In these plays, Shakespeare's poetry becomes more complex. His dialogue is also more dramatic. Today we would call these plays romantic comedies. The comedies were popular with audiences. Some of the more famous comedies are *Much Ado About Nothing* and *As You Like It*.

The next grouping is the tragedies. These are Shakespeare's greatest plays. In the tragedies, Shakespeare wrote his best poetry. He also created some of his most memorable scenes. Have you ever thought about how important these plays are in Western culture? It would be hard to find someone in an English-speaking country who doesn't know the story of *Romeo and Juliet*. Other famous tragedies include *Macbeth, King Lear*, and *Hamlet*.

Shakespeare's plays remain among the most loved in all the world. They have been translated into every major language. They are always being performed all around the world. You can find a listing of all of Shakespeare's plays in the appendix of your textbook.

[Unit 8]

Conversation

Page 86

Practice

W: Hi there. Could I please speak to someone about applying for a position with the student newspaper?

M: Good morning. Yes, I'm the editor of the newspaper; my name is Brian Hall. You can speak to me.

W: Oh, that's great. I'm a second year journalism student here at the school, and I was hoping to get some practical experience working with the newspaper. Are there any positions available at the moment?

M: Actually yes, seeing as it is still the beginning of the year, there are lots of positions available. Would you be looking for a position as a reporter? (*Practice A ends.*)

W: That's right. I'm a good writer. One of my professors last year told me that he saw a lot of merit in an article I wrote for his class.

M: That is great, good for you. Now could you tell me a little about what you know about the student newspaper?

W: Sure thing. I've heard that this newspaper is pretty famous and well known for its thorough research. Its quality and reputation have been a legacy at this school for years. I would very much like to be a part of that.

M: Well it is very nice to know that you do your research! Yes, one of the main functions of the newspaper, as well as to inform, is to unify all of the different students at this school. We strive to be liberal in our views and to appeal to all groups and minorities in the school.

W: It sounds like a great challenge to me. I think it will be exciting to try and write articles that can appeal to every minority as well as the masses without becoming ambiguous.

M: It can be difficult but you must always try to avoid writing a distortion of the truth. Well, you sound as if you know what you are talking about. Why don't you write me a few articles, and we will see if they are good enough for the next edition.

W: That would be perfect. Thank you so much.

Page 88

Test

M: Hi there, Mary. I have an article to submit for tomorrow's edition.

W: Oh, OK, Tom. What is it about? May I see it?

M: Yeah, sure, here it is. It is about the dean of the school and the legacy that he has left behind here. The good and bad sides of it.

W: Oh really? It sounds interesting, but I wonder if it could cause a lot of trouble for the newspaper.

M: Look, I know that this is a school newspaper, but this article has merit and deserves to be shown to the students.

W: All right, wait while I look at it.

M: Sure. I know that the dean was famous for improving the school.

W: Yes, he was able to unify the staff and students and make them proud of this school. He also raised the ratio of students from ethnic minorities here, which has improved the school's reputation even more.

M: Yes, I am aware of that, but as you can see in this part, that is a distortion of what really happened. The dean made sure that every class included a certain number of students from different ethnic minorities. This was only done to raise the overall ratio in the school. His policy was morally ambiguous in my opinion.

W: I can see what you mean, but I think that you have to be very careful not to accuse anyone of anything without evidence. I can see here, though, that not everything in your article is against him. You make some good observations and praise him, too. You can be liberal in your views at times.

M: Yes, I strive to be. The story is balanced and should be seen by everyone.

W: All right, if you make the changes that I have marked down in your article, and provide a little more evidence to back up what you are saying, then we will publish it.

Page 90

Practice

W: Moving water has been used to make power for centuries. Waterwheels were the first method to use the power of moving water. Here's how it works. Gravity moves water down rivers. People place a large wheel partially submerged in the river. The moving water moves the wheel. The moving wheel is what makes energy.

Electricity made by flowing water is called hydroelectricity. This is the type of power made in dams. Hydroelectricity is a clean way of making power. About nineteen percent of the world's annual power comes from dams. This way of making power has been used for over 100 years. On the other hand, tidal stream power is a new way of using water to make energy. This new method also uses moving water and is a clean way of making power. But let's take a look at some differences between the two. (*Practice A ends.*)

Hydroelectricity uses gravity and a river to make energy. Tidal stream power doesn't need a river. Tidal stream power uses the underwater currents in the ocean, which are also affected by gravity. The power in these currents is converted to electricity. Tidal stream power can be made anywhere that there is an ocean—anywhere along a coast. Electricity made by dams can only be made where there is a river.

Some parts of the world have serious droughts. When the water volume in rivers drops, it is difficult to make hydroelectricity. However, there is never a drought in the ocean, so tidal stream power is not affected by weather conditions.

So what can we say? Hydroelectricity is a proven way of making energy. It has been used for centuries. In contrast, tidal stream power is still being developed. It looks like a good alternative, right? But more research will be needed before the substitution of older methods of generating hydroelectricity can occur.

Pages 92–93

Test

W: Last week, we talked about hydroelectric power and tidal stream power. Both of these systems use moving water to make power. Does anyone remember what type of moving water each system uses?

M: Hydroelectric power uses water moved by gravity in rivers. Tidal stream power uses ocean currents caused by gravity. They both convert the energy in moving water into electricity.

W: That's right. Now, let's look at other ways of generating power. Today, we are going to compare water power and wind power. Most energy sources we use today cause pollution. They are also running out. It is important for us to find clean energy substitutions to meet our annual energy needs. And we need energy that is renewable. Renewable energy is energy that will not run out. Wind and water power are both clean renewable energy sources.

M: Then how do we choose which one to use?

W: Good question. Let's take a look at both. Both systems make energy at a low cost. But water power is more predictable. Rivers and currents run every day. The water volume in rivers may change, but it is pretty steady. But the wind doesn't always blow. There may be some days when wind power won't produce energy. Both systems are quiet. But wind power requires towers that many people find ugly. You can see some of these towers near our campus.

M: Yes, I've seen them. They are ugly.

W: Yes, I agree. Let me see, where was I? Water power and wind power both have problems with location. Water power can only be made near rivers or the ocean. Wind power can only be made in places with steady winds. Both systems have environmental concerns. Some birds die by running into the towers built to make wind power. This is a big worry in areas with rare types of birds. Most types of water power need a dam. Some people worry that dams damage the environment. Finally, both systems can be expensive to install. Building towers for wind power is expensive. And, of course, building a dam costs a lot.

Now, back to your question. How do we choose between water and wind power?

M: It seems like it depends on where you are.

W: Yes, location is a big concern. How about for our campus, what type of system would you choose?

M: It is windy here a lot. But there are also two big rivers nearby. The mountains here are windy, but the trees are beautiful. The contrast of the trees against the wind towers would be ugly. I think I would choose water power because I don't like the way wind power towers look.

Transcripts

[Unit 9]

Conversation

Pages 96–97

Practice

M: Good morning professor. How are you today?

W: Hello, James. I am very well, thank you. Have a seat, and let's have a look at your thesis.

M: Thanks. I have been worrying about this feedback all week.

W: I understand that it can be a worrying time for students, but most of the hard work is over now that the exams have finished.

M: That is true. I have to admit that I am relieved now.

W: Now, your thesis was about the ways in which advertising can affect the way people think about products, was it not?

M: That is correct. I think that I did quite a good job with it.

W: Well yes, overall it was quite a good thesis. (*Practice A ends.*) However, there were a couple of issues with it that I need to address.

M: All right.

W: At times in the paper, you seemed to have some difficulties putting your ideas in words. You struggled to get your point across clearly, but most of the time your ideas were concise and demonstrated a lot of insight.

M: I am glad to hear that. At times, I did have some trouble expressing my ideas clearly.

W: Yes, it is important to back up everything that you say in any thesis.

M: Absolutely, I can see that now.

W: Also, occasionally, you still made a few mistakes with your grammar and spelling, which is a rather careless thing to do in such an important assignment. It means that my overall assessment of your work is not as good as it could have been. Just because of a few simple spelling errors.

M: I understand. Unfortunately, I was running out of time as the deadline for the thesis approached.

W: I can see that. Overall it was a good paper, though, and you received a B plus mark for it. Well done.

M: Thank you, professor. Goodbye.

Page 98

Test

W: Excuse me, professor. Do you have some time to spare? I'd like to speak to you.

M: Come in, Sarah. These are my office hours. I'm not going anywhere.

W: Oh great! I have just completed a full draft of my history essay, which is due next week. I was hoping that you could have a look at it and give me a little feedback on it if possible?

M: I'm sure that wouldn't be a problem. Now let's have a look at it.

W: Sure, thank you. Here you go. This is the first time that I have completed an assignment like this so early.

M: Well, just as long as you remember that is not necessarily a good thing. Did you give enough thought to it all? I'm looking for your critical insights as part of my assessment. How long have you spent writing the piece?

W: I can happily admit that I have done a great deal of research and have spent a long time, carefully writing it. I'm quite proud of it really.

M: OK, that's great to hear. I can see here that you have followed the directions. It looks as though you have done as asked. The historical evidence has been linked together by your own ideas. This is impressive.

W: Oh my goodness, I am so relieved to hear that.

M: I can see here that, occasionally you lose your place and can become side-tracked. That's a struggle in writing that many students face. You should be careful not to lose sight of the message you are trying to get across.

W: Thank you, professor. I will address that.

M: Good. So after a quick look over this paper, I would say that it is concise and well written. You just have to make sure that you do not go off-track in your writing.

W: Thank you again, professor. I can't tell you how relieved I am that I do not have to start all over again!

M: Ha, nothing of the sort. In fact, if your thesis is this organized and well written, you will do very well, Sarah. Good luck.

Pages 100–101

Practice

W: There are different theories used to explain human behavior. Psychology has a number of schools. Each school has a different ideology. But each school has some overlap with the others. The schools of psychoanalysis and behaviorism are quite old. Two newer schools of thought are the cognitive and humanistic schools of psychology.

Psychoanalysis is the most famous of the schools. This school says we do things because of our internal thoughts. We do things because of thoughts we aren't aware of. How many of you have felt angry or depressed and not known why? Yes, I think we all have. This is evidence that we do things because of thoughts that we are not aware of. (*Practice A ends.*) Behaviorism is a very different school. It claims that what you think is unimportant. People do things because of rewards and punishment. How many of you study hard because you want an A? Yes, I see some of you aren't studying too hard. This is evidence that we do things because of rewards. On the other hand, humanists reject both psychoanalysis and behaviorism. They believe we do things because of our values and choices. How many of you don't steal because you think it is wrong? Yes, most of us choose not to steal because we feel it is wrong. Even when we know we won't get caught, most of us don't steal. This is evidence that we do things because of our values and choices.

Cognitive psychologists look at thinking. They believe we do things because of our reasoning and thinking. How many of you think you get good grades because you work hard? OK, now how many of you think you get good grades because of your intelligence? Cognitive psychologists would say that you have an opinion about yourself because you have thought about it. This is evidence that you are able to reason or think about why you do well in school.

Pages 102–103

Test

M: Previously we talked about different theories in psychology. There are many different ideas about why people do things. The ideologies of each school of psychology were covered in the last lecture. But actually, all of these theories may soon change. A new kind of technology called a "neuro-chip" may change the way people's brains work.

W: Neuro-chip. That sounds like something from a movie.

M: Ha, ha yes! But this is real. Scientists have found a way to combine a living thing and a computer chip. A neuro-chip is part brain cells and part computer chip. A neuro-chip is made from a 1-millimeter square computer chip and some brain cells. And such a neuro-chip could be placed inside a living brain.

W: Does that mean the person would be part computer?

M: In a way. The living cell and the computer chip would be able to communicate with each other. This is an exciting breakthrough. The neuro-chip has two potential uses. The first use will probably be to build super fast computers. It won't happen for years. But researchers think they can build "living" computers that will be much faster than today's computers. But for this class, we are more interested in the second use. Neuro-chips could be used to treat human diseases.

W: Could the neuro-chip be used to replace a person's brain and improve our intelligence?

M: I don't think we will ever replace an entire brain. There would always be some overlap between the natural brain and the neuro-chips. But someday neuro-chips might replace damaged parts of a person's brain and restore their cognitive abilities. There still needs to be a lot of research done. But someday it could be possible to take a damaged brain and make it work normally again.

W: What kind of diseases could be cured with neuro-chips?

M: Let's look at the simplest example. Nerves send messages from your brain to your body. They also send information from your body to your brain. An injured nerve means a person may not be able to use part of their body. For example, a person who cannot walk may have injured nerves in their back.

W: Could neuro-chips help them to walk again?

M: Possibly. Neuro-chips might be placed where the nerve was damaged. Then the messages from the brain could reach the person's legs and they could walk. This is very exciting research.

W: Do neuro-chips have any uses in psychology?

M: Possibly. A person who has depression might have part of their brain that is less or more active. Neuro-chips could be placed in the brain to make that part of their brain work better.

[Unit 10]

Conversation

Pages 106–107

Practice

M: Hello, Professor Jones. Do you have a few minutes?

W: I'm quite busy actually. I have a meeting at the Publishing Practitioners' Organization later, but I can spare a few minutes. What can I do for you?

M: Well, it's coming toward the end of the year, and I am worried about my low grade in class. Is there anything that I can do to gain extra credit?

W: It's good you are concerned about this. You have been distracted from your studies, and your marks have begun to lag behind others in your class.

M: Yes, I have had some problems at home, but they are over. I have been a little passive. I should have pushed myself to do better. (*Practice A ends.*) But I would really like to make up for that, now. What are my options?

W: Fortunately, as you have realized this before the final push at the end of the year has commenced, there is still a chance for you to get a slight increase in your grade by doing some work for extra credit.

M: That is good. Is there a job I could get? Or perhaps I could do an extra assignment for it?

W: There is extra work I could assign for you to catch up with the rest of the class. I think, though, that it would be beneficial for you to get some practical experience.

M: That would be ideal for me. How can I go about finding work and what's the scope of jobs I can look for?

W: Well, as it is for credit, it would have to be organized through me. In fact, my meeting with the Publishing Practitioners' Organization later is regarding a paper that I am writing. I am looking for help with some of my empirical research. In helping with that, you would be warranted to receive extra credit for it and reduce your credit deficit. It would certainly help to raise your standing in the class higher than intermediate. Is that OK?

M: That would be wonderful, professor. Thanks!

Page 108

Test

W: Excuse me, Professor Andrews. May I speak with you?

M: Certainly, Lisa. Come in and have a seat. Now what would you like to talk about?

W: Well, there are a couple of things actually. I know that we have commenced with my program of extra work to make up for my credit deficit, but I was hoping that I could have an extra week to write the current paper.

M: Uh oh, Lisa. This is not good at all, not again. It had better be warranted this time.

W: I'm sorry, professor. I really am. I have two other exams to take at the end of this week, and I am worried that if I do not focus on them, I will not do well. That could make me lag behind even further.

M: OK, I can understand that within the scope of all your coursework you may not be able to carry out extra work every week, but you must give me more notice than this. Now what exams do you have?

W: I have a really hard physics test coming up. We have to analyze a lot of empirical data and write an essay for that test. Then I have this thing called a "practitioner's exam" in chemistry. We have to actually do an experiment right there on the spot! For both of those tests, I'll need to prepare really well.

M: You have already been too passive in making up your credit deficit. How do you expect to get a good job in the science field when you are distracted from your work every other week?

W: I'm sorry, professor, but I really am trying hard now to pull myself above an intermediate level with my grades. I realize that I have been a bit lazy in the past and want to change that. I promise I will not make any more mistakes like this.

M: OK Lisa, you may hand in your paper next week. But if I get the slightest feeling that you are not taking this extra work seriously, I will stop giving it to you and you will fail the class. Understood?

W: Understood, professor. Thank you.

Pages 110–111

Practice

M: Most of us use our computers every day. I know I couldn't get anything done without my computer. Our computers are only as good as their memory. Of course, it isn't that simple. Computer memory is analogous to human memory in some ways, but how it works is very different. The first memory systems were quite simple. Actually, the first computer memory system was built in 1834.

W: I didn't know there were computers then.

M: This wasn't a true computer. It was a manual system. And it wasn't very useful. It'll be more useful for us to focus on three modern memory systems. Each system is different from the others. And each system improved on earlier systems. Let's look at these systems—drum memory, magnetic core memory, and semiconductor memory—in chronological order. (*Practice A ends.*) The first in the sequence is "drum memory." This system was invented in 1932. It used a drum to record data. A substance on the drum recorded data. This was the earliest memory system used with modern computers, but it was not used for long. It was replaced by a magnetic system. The next memory system was magnetic core memory. This system used ceramic rings. These rings stored memory using a magnetic field. It was invented in 1947. This system made other computers obsolete.

W: Which of these types of memory does my computer use?

M: The computers we use don't use either of these systems. The norm today is semiconductor memory. Computer chips store the memory. This is called random-access memory or RAM. This was a big change in computer memory. Before RAM, data could only be read in the same sequence that it was recorded. RAM allowed data to be read in any sequence.

Pages 112–113

Test

M: We've been talking about the history of computer memory. We discussed three main types of computer memory. Does anyone remember what they are?

W: I think they were drum, magnetic core, and semiconductor.

M: Yes. That's right. Before that, the first memory system was a manual system developed in 1834. However, for modern memory systems computer memory has moved from, in chronological order, drum, to magnetic to semiconductor. Of course the norm today is semiconductor memory. Today, we are going to talk about an exciting development in computers. Who has heard of nanotechnology?

W: I've heard of it. Doesn't it have to do with things that are very small?

M: That's right. Nano means small. Nanotechnology is technology that is very small. It is so small that we can't see it without a microscope. There are many possible uses of this new technology. Computers are one. But, in fact, there are four types of nanocomputers that could be built. One is an electronic computer. These would be the closest to the computers we use today. These computers would use tiny circuits that are analogous to today's computers. Other nanocomputers could be chemical or even living. These computers would work through the interactions of chemicals. To make chemical nanocomputers, single atoms would be used to store data. Individual atoms would also be used to solve problems. These computers would have many uses. Some researchers in Scotland are trying to make computers that could be placed on the skin. These computers could check the person's health and call for help if there was a problem. Another kind, mechanical nanocomputers, would use tiny moving pieces. These pieces are called "nanogears." Nanogears would store data and solve problems. Many researchers think that these tiny computers could be used to control a nanorobot.

W: Does that mean what I think it does?

M: Yes, tiny robots. These robots could be used to attack diseases in the body. Cancer is a good example. They could be programmed to find cancer cells and kill them. The last type of nanocomputer is quantum nanocomputers. These computers would use the laws of physics to store data and solve problems. These computers could be the fastest computers ever built. They could also be the most powerful. These are really the most exciting of the nanocomputers. They could solve problems that none of today's computers can. Nanocomputers may change the way we live our lives. Many people think that in the near future computers will be in everything from our clothes to our bodies. We don't know in what sequence these computers will be developed. But they will come soon.

[Unit 11]

Conversation

Pages 116–117

Practice

W: Justin, I need to speak with you. Do you have a few minutes?

M: Yeah. I have a break between classes. I hope everything is OK.

W: Actually, I have a few concerns about your last paper.

M: Oh no. Did I do a bad job?

W: Well, your paper was very similar to a research paper that is available on the Internet. Do you have anything to say about that?

M: I don't understand. Are you asking me if I plagiarized? (*Practice A ends.*)

W: Yes Justin. We take plagiarism very seriously. There are severe repercussions for such actions.

M: I used the Internet to research the paper, but I didn't think I was plagiarizing.

W: Well any degree of copying is considered plagiarizing, and it appears you copied a lot. Whenever you use information from a publication or from the Internet, you must show that you are quoting it and not make it look like it is your own work.

M: I see. I didn't realize that.

W: Well the instructions on how to cite information and the rules about copying were quite clear in the handbook I gave you at the beginning of the semester.

M: Can't I just take a failing grade for the paper or delete the passages I used from the Internet?

W: No, a rule is a rule. Unfortunately, you will get a failing grade in the class and most likely suspension from the university.

M: [*Panicked.*] Suspension from the university? What does that mean?

W: You will not be able to attend this university for at least four semesters. There have been several cases where students have been expelled from the university.

M: Oh no! I don't know what to say. . .

Page 118

Test

M: Professor Belle, do you have a few minutes?

W: I have a few minutes.

M: I am reading the student handbook, and I have a few questions on the section that talks about plagiarism.

W: I am glad to know someone is reading this handbook. All students could benefit from reading it. What are your questions?

M: Well my first question is what is considered plagiarism? I don't understand what the passage is describing on plagiarism.

W: That is a good question. A lot of students seem not to understand plagiarism very well. Plagiarism is any thought or written work of another, claimed by someone else as his or her own original work. Many students don't realize you have to give recognition to an author's thoughts or written work.

M: Does it matter how much of a thought or amount of written work you use?

W: Any amount needs to be cited or documented in your research paper or speech.

M: Even if it is just a sentence?

W: Yes, Henry.

M: The handbook also mentions plagiarism could lead to suspension. How long are students usually suspended?

W: The average student who has been caught plagiarizing is suspended for about four semesters. There are several cases where the student is expelled.

M: Whoa! Expulsion is a severe repercussion. . .

W: Plagiarism is taken very seriously, Henry. That is why there are such severe consequences.

M: Is there a writing center I can take my research papers to have them checked for plagiarism?

W: There is a writing center where you can have someone look over your paper. Also, you can sit down with your professor to look over your paper, if they have time. When in doubt, cite or quote the original author.

M: Thanks, Professor Belle. I think I'm going to start taking plagiarism a bit more seriously.

Page 120

Practice

M: How many of you have heard of NATO? Yes. We have all heard of NATO. NATO is one of the most important organizations in the world. After WWII, the world was divided. The United States was on one side and the USSR on the other. Many countries at the time sought to make defense alliances. Then, in 1948, several European nations signed the Treaty of Brussels, agreeing to come to the aid of the others. The treaty made the Western European Union. This was a military alliance. However, this alliance was not as powerful as the USSR. The Europeans knew they needed the participation of America. (*Practice A ends.*) The next year, NATO was formed. The US, Canada, and most of Western Europe formed NATO. NATO was made to stop any threat from the USSR.

W: How could NATO stop the USSR?

M: That's a good question. The USSR had a powerful military. To stop it, all of NATO would have to work together. Article 5 was at the heart of NATO. It states that all nations agree to defend each other. Now, when NATO was formed, both sides had mostly conventional forces. This soon changed. In the 1950s, both sides began a buildup of nuclear weapons. Each side soon had the ability to destroy the other. This situation led to the strategy of Mutually Assured Destruction (MAD). If either side attacked, the outcome would have been a nuclear war. Such a war would end with mutual destruction. This nuclear standoff held for forty years. There was never a war between NATO and the USSR. Then the USSR collapsed in 1990. NATO is still an important military alliance, albeit less important than in the past. Today, NATO is in the process of redefining itself.

Pages 122–123

Test

M: We're continuing our discussion of NATO today. We said it was an alliance between the US, Canada, and Western Europe. Of course, the USSR had a similar alliance. It was called the Warsaw Pact. Does anyone remember why NATO was formed?

W: It was formed as protection.

M: That's right. Protection from what?

W: Countries in Western Europe sought protection from the USSR.

M: That's right. Western Europe was afraid of an attack from the USSR. The USSR and Eastern Europe were also afraid that NATO would attack them. They wanted mutual protection. They formed the Warsaw Pact, albeit, six years after NATO was formed. The Warsaw Pact was modeled after NATO.

W: You said that NATO forces never fought the USSR. Did they ever fight the Warsaw Pact?

M: No. NATO and Warsaw Pact forces never fought. There were actually a few times that they were on the same side. Canadian and Polish forces were both part of UN forces a few times.

W: There must have been a lot of money spent for protection that wasn't used.

M: Actually, Warsaw Pact troops were used but not against NATO. They were twice used against other Warsaw Pact nations.

W: How could they have fought against themselves?

M: The first time was in 1956. Hungary tried to leave the Warsaw Pact. The USSR demanded their participation. USSR forces invaded Hungary. The outcome was never in doubt. The fighting lasted just two weeks. Hungary was forced to stay in the Warsaw Pact. Later, Warsaw Pact forces invaded another member nation in 1968. This time Czechoslovakia was invaded. Almost all of the forces were from the USSR. The fighting was over quickly.

W: Why would they invade countries they were supposed to protect?

M: The USSR dominated all of its allies. They used the Warsaw Pact to control the other countries in it.

W: What does the Warsaw Pact do today?

M: The Warsaw Pact ended in 1991. The members decided that they didn't want the USSR to protect them anymore.

W: Does each country protect itself now?

M: Many of the countries that were in the Warsaw Pact are now in NATO. NATO is now made of almost every country in Europe plus the US and Canada.

[Unit 12]

Conversation

Page 126

Practice

W: Thanks for taking the time to meet with me, Mr. Kovach.

M: No problem, Alexi. It is my understanding you want to talk to me in regards to the recreation facility.

W: Yes, and also the snack bar adjoining the recreation facility. I hope to get the hours changed. (*Practice A ends.*)

M: The hours?

W: The hours that they are open and available to students. Right now, the recreation facility opens at 7 a.m. and closes at 9 p.m. and the snack bar is only open on intramural game days.

M: What do you propose?

W: It would be great to have the recreation facility stay open until ten. That would give the students who have evening classes a chance to get to the gym. As for the snack bar, it would also be great if it were open during the peak hours of the afternoon. I believe it would make money during those hours.

M: Alexi, you have some valid points, but I do not make the decisions to keep these facilities open. However, I will be able to arrange an appointment for you to sit with the Sites and Facilities Committee. They are the committee that makes the decisions having to do with what you want to change.

W: How soon will I be able to meet with them? I would like to see some changes commence by the end of the spring semester.

M: Don't worry. They meet twice a month, and luckily, they will be meeting at the beginning of next week. I will set you up to meet with them then.

W: Great.

M: If you leave your phone number with my secretary, I will call you with specifics.

W: Thanks again, Mr. Kovach, for your help.

M: I don't feel like I was able to help you all that much, but you're welcome.

Page 128

Test

M: Good morning, Ms. Hinkle!

W: Good morning, Brandon. How did your meeting go yesterday?

M: It was really good.

W: I heard a few members from the Sites and Facility Committee speaking, and they said they have given permission to the Student Activities Club to use the courtyard for concerts this spring.

M: Yes, but it took a long time to finally get the committee to agree with what the students had to say.

W: How did you manage to convince them?

M: We approached them with a written proposal and several valid reasons.

W: Sounds like you were well prepared.

M: We were very prepared. We really want to have more fun activities, like concerts, for students.

W: How many concerts do you want to try to host?

M: We hope at least five.

W: When are the concerts scheduled to begin?

M: This spring. However, we need to find a university employee who wants to sponsor the concerts.

W: What are the commitments?

M: To be the university employee representative at our meetings. We hold meetings twice a month.

W: If that is all that is asked of a sponsor, I think I could fill that role.

M: Really?

W: Sure. I will gladly be your university employee sponsor. Just e-mail me the details of what I need to know and where I need to be.

M: This is great! Thank you so much, Ms. Hinkle. I think you are going to enjoy this.

W: Me, too! Well Brandon, I have to get moving to my next class. Congratulations on this, and I look forward to the first meeting.

M: Thanks again, and I will get you the information this afternoon.

Page 130

Practice

M: Method acting became popular in New York City in the 1930s. This approach to acting tries to get the actor to feel real emotions. Method acting is really several schools of acting. All of these schools have the same goal. They use the actor's emotions to bring intensity to their acting. Let's take a look at some of the different method acting approaches and what results they give.

The most famous method acting school was the Actors' Studio. The teachers at this school told actors to use real emotions from their past. Actors were also encouraged to think of the character as a real person. In a scene, a character might be angry. The actor would think of a time when he or she was angry. This anger would then be displayed in the scene, often in a dramatic fashion. This method helps many actors lose their inhibitions. (*Practice A ends.*)

In another approach, actors use their imagination. In this approach, actors imagine themselves as the character. This transformation helps the actor understand the character's wants and needs. The actors then imagine themselves to be their characters. They imagine that they have the same wants and needs. This way the emotions become real for the actor. In a scene, the character might need to convince a judge of his innocence. The actor would imagine that he really needed to convince the judge. This way the scene would be more realistic. The emotions would be real.

Another approach also encouraged actors to use their imagination. This approach encouraged actors to imagine situations. A character might need to be happy in a scene. The actor would imagine a happy situation. As with the previous two approaches, the goal is to make the emotions real.

Pages 132-133

Test

W: Let's review what we've learned about method acting. Remember, in method acting, actors tried to bring emotional intensity to their scenes. There were three ways actors did this. First, they used their past emotions. Second, they imagined themselves as the character. Finally, they imagined situations where they would feel a certain emotion. Today we are going to talk about a different approach to acting.

"Viewpoints" is an approach to acting that doesn't involve emotions. Method acting made everyone think about emotions and acting. Actors wanted to lose their inhibitions and display emotions. Some acting teachers thought actors were forgetting other parts of acting. They wanted to teach acting that wasn't emotion. So, while lots of teachers were focusing on emotion, others began to look at four "viewpoints."

The first viewpoint was space. Space refers to dramatic space. There are three parts to it. First is the shape of the stage or movie set. The second is the space between an actor and other things. Actors need to be aware of the space between themselves and other actors and objects. The last type of space is called the floor pattern. This refers to the actor's movement. OK, the second viewpoint is shape. This is the shape of the actor's body.

M: Does this mean that actors should exercise more?

W: Ha ha, no. This means that actors should be aware of how they stand and move. It also means that actors should make their movements seem real. To show anger, they should appear angry like a real person. They shouldn't appear too angry. They should look as angry as people do in real life.

The next viewpoint is time. Time also has three parts to it. It is how fast or slow something happens. Also, it is how long something lasts. And it is the repetition of something. The fourth and final viewpoint is movement. This is the way actors move their bodies. Do they move smoothly, or do they move in jerks?

M: This seems like a lot for an actor to think about.

W: Yes it is. And it takes some time for actors to understand it. But once they understand it, it can cause a transformation in their acting. Before we go, let's look at the last part of viewpoints. For viewpoints to work, it must all fit together. This is what you were asking about. Actors must work on each viewpoint by itself. Then they can bring them all together. Once they bring all four elements together, that is when the transformation happens.

M: So all of this came about because some teachers thought there was too much focus on emotion in acting?

W: That's right.

Transcripts

[Review 2]

Conversation 1

Page 135

W: Excuse me, Professor Jackson. Do you have a minute?

M: I do for my best student, yes.

W: I don't know about that.

M: Don't be so modest. What can I do for you today?

W: Well, incredible as it seems, I will be graduating this year. I'm currently looking at applying to graduate schools, and I wondered if you would be able to write me a letter of recommendation.

M: It would be my pleasure to write a recommendation on your behalf. In fact, it will be nice to write one where all my comments are genuine for a change, as you are a great student.

W: Well, I'm applying to five different programs, so hopefully I'll get into at least one of them. These are the forms you need to fill out. Some of them require somewhat explicit answers. It seems pretty straightforward though. None of the questions seem to be ambiguous.

M: OK. Well, while you're here, let me locate your file and make sure I have everything I need to complete the forms. . . Ah, here it is. OK, I seem to have everything here. What type of programs are you applying to? Are they all programs to do with liberal studies?

W: Three of them are. Two of them are education programs.

M: Ah, education. You are doing a minor in that, aren't you?

W: Yes, liberal studies is my major, but I have been taking education classes as well. There's actually quite a lot of overlap between the two courses.

M: OK, well why don't you give me a couple of days to complete these forms? Then, I'll email you and let you know that I got everything done and sent off.

W: That sounds great. Thank you for taking the time to see me and for writing my letter of recommendation.

M: Anytime. Good luck with your applications. Let me know the outcome.

Lecture 1

Pages 136-137

W: Researchers have empirical evidence that a healthy lifestyle can help you live longer. They estimate that if you convert to a healthy lifestyle, you can live about fifteen to twenty years longer. This is an incredible increase. Most of the behaviors associated with a healthy lifestyle are easy to do. These life extending behaviors can be placed into four categories. The first category is some behaviors you shouldn't do. What things shouldn't you do if you want to live a long life?

M: You shouldn't smoke.

W: Yes. Smoking is probably the single most damaging thing you can do to your body. It is a known cause of cancer. It also causes many other diseases. If you smoke, you should stop now. Drinking large amounts of alcohol is another thing you shouldn't do. Also, you shouldn't eat a lot of processed foods. These foods have a lot of refined sugar in them. Refined sugar has been shown to speed up the lifecycle of the body's cells. This makes the cells die faster, and this means you die sooner. And the last thing is to avoid dangerous situations. Don't take part in activities where you might die by accident.

The second category is things you should eat. Tied for number one on the list of things you should eat are fruits and vegetables. These foods are full of antioxidants that protect your body's cells. You should also eat fish such as salmon. Surprisingly, you should eat dark chocolate and drink small amounts of alcohol. Dark chocolate has substances that protect your heart and blood vessels. Other types of chocolate are not good for you. And in a seeming contradiction, a small amount of alcohol daily, such as red wine, is good for your heart.

The next category is no surprise, but is difficult for many of us to do: exercise. Exercising daily even for short periods has been shown to greatly extend a person's life. Also, the type of exercise you do doesn't have to be of high intensity.

The last category is lifestyle. This group of behaviors has some surprises. Having a regular sleep schedule is an important aspect of health that many people ignore. Depression has been shown to shorten a person's life, so be optimistic. Remaining cognitively active and having friends has also been shown to help people live longer.

These behaviors are easy to do. With a little effort, we can all live longer.

Lecture 2

Pages 138-139

W: Today we will talk about fairy tales. The most famous fairy tale writers are the Grimm Brothers'. They wrote many of the most widely read fairy tales in the Western world. Does anyone know any of the Brothers Grimm stories?

M: *Snow White* and *Cinderella*. But weren't those stories only written down by the brothers?

W: You're right. The Brothers Grimm weren't story writers at all. They were academics. How many of you have heard of some Brothers Grimms' stories? As I thought, almost everyone has. The stories are read all over the world.

M: How did two academics end up so famous for children's stories?

W: The Grimm Brothers' were born in the late 1700s. They were born in what is today Germany. As academics, the brothers studied language. Well, maybe I should say they sought to study language. But they ended up finding genuine masterpieces in folk tales. These stories have spread all over the world. This is an outcome they couldn't have predicted, albeit a fortunate one.

M: How did the stories spread?

W: This process began with the brothers listening to language. They traveled to different towns to listen to the local speech. They wanted to study the speech of people in different towns. The people in the towns told the brothers local fairy tales. The brothers wrote down the stories to avoid distortion of the peoples' speech. Over time the brothers collected many stories.

Then they published them in a book for children. The first book of stories wasn't very popular. But they published a second book a few years later. All together, there were 156 stories in the two books. The second book became quite popular. It's interesting that the Grimm Brothers' thought of the stories as academic not as entertaining.

M: So, the Brothers Grimm wrote down stories to study language. They then published these stories, and they became popular?

W: Yes. The stories have become popular in many cultures. The first English translation of the stories was made in 1823. That was less than ten years after they were published in German. Since then, the stories have been translated into every major language in the world. Many of the stories have also been made into movies. These wonderful stories are still enjoyed by children today.

Lecture 3

Pages 140-141

M: Today we are going to talk about the effects of a disaster and the steps the Red Cross took to respond to that disaster. In 2007, Mexico experienced massive flooding. Flooding in parts of Mexico is almost an annual event. But this was one of the worst natural disasters in Mexico's history. Has anyone heard about these floods?

W: Yes. I have some family who live there. It was very bad for them.

M: Yes. They were some of the worst floods in Mexico's history. Two factors contributed to the flooding. Flood control measures had been planned. But they had not been completed. In 2007, the area experienced five days of heavy rain. The heavy rain and lack of flood control resulted in the flooding. Over a million people were affected by the flood waters. Many of them were left homeless.

The president of Mexico flew over the flooded area. He could only see the red rooftops of the houses. The flood waters were covering everything else. The hospitals and schools were closed. 69,000 people were housed in shelters. Another 100,000 were wandering the streets without shelter. The destruction was incredible. Many people thought the devastation was analogous to a war zone.

Transcripts

The International Red Cross and Mexican Red Cross brought a coherent response to the situation. The first problem was what to do with 100,000 homeless people. The Red Cross began to evacuate people to safer areas. Many people were brought to other states, even as far away as Mexico City.

During the flood, many family members had been separated from their loved ones. The Red Cross began working on "family linking." Through these efforts, thousands of people were reunited with their family members.

Of course, since the hospitals were closed, medical services were needed. The Red Cross setup temporary medical centers in many communities. They also sent mobile teams out to find injured or sick people. This concise effort helped thousands of people.

Most people in the area had little or no food. The Red Cross moved quickly to give supplies to people in need. Within a short time people in the area were safe and being taken care of.

Of course, the Red Cross was only part of the aid story. The people of Mexico were generous in giving aid. The EU, the US, and Canada also gave to the relief effort.

Conversation 2

Page 142

M: Hello. I need to speak to someone about getting some financial assistance. I've never sought this kind of help before. Have I come to the right place?

W: Well, are you a student here? If you are, then you've come to the right place, as we offer financial assistance to students of this university, but not the general public.

M: Great! I'm a student here.

W: Then, how can I help you?

M: I've gotten behind in my rent, and I need a loan to pay it so that I don't lose my apartment.

W: It sounds like you might be eligible for an emergency student loan. I need to ask you a few questions to get us started. Is that OK?

M: Sure.

W: How much do you want to borrow?

M: About $300.

W: Do you have a job? And if so, what's your annual income?

M: Yes. I work part-time at the fruit shop on campus, but I'm not really sure what I earn in a year.

W: That's OK. What I really need to know is if we can organize this loan. How long do you think it would take you to pay it back?

M: Mmm. . . I think it will take me about three months to earn enough money to pay it back.

W: OK. Well, to be eligible for an emergency student loan, you need to have a genuine and valid reason to apply for the loan, apply for less than $500, be employed, and be able to pay the whole loan back in full within six months. Fortunately, your situation fits that description.

M: Great, my apartment owner will be really happy.

W: OK. Well here are the forms you need to complete to commence the loan application. Let me know if you need any help with them.

M: Thank you.

Answer Key

[Unit 1]

Conversation

Pages 8–9

A

1. B   2. A

B

Woman - Student	Man - Professor
• Decided to <u>change her degree</u> • Asking about <u>subjects in the Communication Degree</u> • Doesn't enjoy <u>the course she is studying now</u> • <u>Thinks it sounds like a great degree</u> • <u>Has a better idea of what she wants to do now</u>	• Will have to <u>attend a bridging course</u> • Course looks at <u>advertising, public relations, and marketing</u> • Will also study <u>the theory</u> • <u>There will be ongoing work experience</u> • <u>Will have to do a lot of studying</u> • <u>Hopes the student makes the right decision</u>

C

1. A   2. A   3. B

D

1. attend   2. ongoing   3. criteria
4. consult   5. incorporate

Page 10

Man - Student	Woman - Professor
• Considering <u>signing up for the graphic design class</u> • Wants to know <u>how the course is graded</u> • <u>Likes that there is no big exam at the end of the class</u> • <u>Will find out about marketing and public relations classes, too</u> • <u>Will get back to her tomorrow</u>	• Has a <u>copy of the class syllabus</u> • Class made up of <u>written work, individual projects, and ongoing classroom assessments</u> • <u>Class is too short to offer work experience</u> • <u>Students must attend forty percent of classes</u>

1. C   2. A
3. C   4. Yes, No, Yes, No

Lecture

Pages 12–13

A

1. A   2. B   3. B   4. C

B and C

Underlined answers from part B.

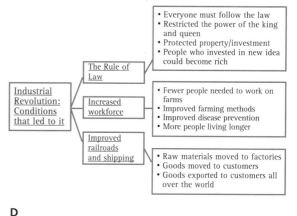

D

1. A   2. A   3. A

E

1. restrict   2. migration   3. revolution
4. exports   5. workforce

Pages 14–15

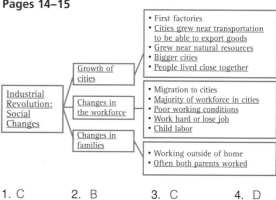

1. C   2. B   3. C   4. D
5. C   6. Yes, Yes, No, No, Yes

Check-up

Page 16

A

1. A   2. D

B

1. raw material   2. industry   3. fortune
4. work experience 5. workshop   6. Bridge
7. industrial   8. Marketing
9. textiles   10. public relations

[Unit 2]

Conversation

Pages 18–19

A

1. B   2. B

B

Man - Student	Woman - University Employee
• Would like to <u>extend his stay in student accommodation over summer</u> • Staying in <u>apartment 104 in the central building</u> • Will go into <u>his final year at university after the summer</u> • <u>Wants to keep the same room and apartment over the summer and for the next year</u>	• Students can extend but <u>it depends on their reason</u> • The apartments are <u>very desirable</u> • Would not have to <u>pay another deposit to keep the apartment</u> • <u>Will make sure that the student can extend his stay</u>

C

1. A   2. A   3. B

D

1. administrate   2. locate   3. somewhat
4. input   5. initial

Page 20

Woman - Student	Man - University Employee
• Is an <u>overseas student from Spain</u> • Going to <u>stay for another semester</u> • Wants to know <u>if she can get student accommodation again</u> • Her last apartment was <u>too small</u> • <u>Wants to use first deposit on the new apartment</u>	• Needs to see <u>student card</u> • It is easier <u>to change apartments than keep an old one</u> • <u>Many students like to keep their apartments</u> • <u>Takes time to organize deposits</u> • <u>Has a bigger apartment, but rent and deposit are higher</u> • <u>Can move in a week before the next semester</u>

1. B   2. C   3. D   4. A

Lecture

Pages 22–23

A

1. B   2. A   3. A   4. C

B and C

Underlined answers from part B.

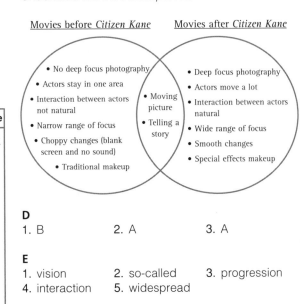

Movies before *Citizen Kane*   Movies after *Citizen Kane*

• No deep focus photography
• Actors stay in one area
• Interaction between actors not natural
• Narrow range of focus
• Choppy changes (blank screen and no sound)
• Traditional makeup

• Moving picture
• Telling a story

• Deep focus photography
• Actors move a lot
• Interaction between actors natural
• Wide range of focus
• Smooth changes
• Special effects makeup

D

1. B   2. A   3. A

E

1. vision   2. so-called   3. progression
4. interaction   5. widespread

Pages 24–25

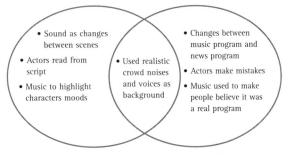

Use of sound in *Citizen Kane*   Use of sound in *War of the Worlds*

• Sound as changes between scenes
• Actors read from script
• Music to highlight characters moods

• Used realistic crowd noises and voices as background

• Changes between music program and news program
• Actors make mistakes
• Music used to make people believe it was a real program

1. D   2. C   3. C   4. A
5. D   6. B

Check-up

Page 26

A

1. C   2. B

B

1. set   2. choppy   3. Narrow
4. focus   5. special effects 6. student card
7. deposit   8. As a matter of fact
9. desirable 10. establish

[Unit 3]

Conversation

Pages 28–29

A

1. A   2. A

B

Man - Student	Woman - Employee
• Confirmed two <u>interviews yesterday</u> • <u>Is wondering about the internships</u>	• Asks if he has <u>prearranged any interviews</u> • There are quite a few <u>people interviewing</u> • Quite a few <u>people get internships from conventions</u> • She estimates <u>85% of students get internships before their final year</u> • <u>Asks him to fill out a form to help with research</u>

C

1. B   2. A   3. B

D

1. supervisor   2. conventions   3. internship
4. estimate   5. confirm

Page 30

Woman - Student	Man - University Employee
• Is looking for the career office because <u>her advisor said it is a place to look for a job</u>. • Her major is <u>architecture</u> • Had an internship <u>the past two summers at an architecture firm</u> • <u>Is graduating this spring</u> • <u>Would like to stay in the city</u>	• Definitely can help • Can arrange a time to <u>see a career counselor</u> • 70% of <u>students who come in get jobs</u> • <u>She has an advantage because she has had internships the past two summers</u> • <u>Good architecture program, so good job placement</u> • <u>Her appointment is at 3</u>

1. C   2. A   3. B   4. A

Lecture

Pages 32–33

A

1. A   2. A   3. B   4. B

B and C

Underlined answers from part B.

Genome Science

Problem	Solution
Running out of energy	→ Make bio-fuel—bacteria to use as fuel
Pollution	→ Make bacteria that will eat pollution—only eat a desired pollutant
Bacteria	→ Make bacteria that will give an early warning of toxins

D

1. A   2. A   3. B

E

1. highlight   2. dispose   3. manipulation
4. mechanism   5. detected

Pages 34–35

Genome DNA Research

Problem	Solution
DNA in the body can cause disease	→ Run tests to see if a person has the DNA then turn off bit of DNA that causes disease <u>for example in cancer</u>
<u>DNA in bacteria causes some disease</u>	→ <u>Turn off DNA in bacteria to kill disease</u>
<u>DNA in viruses causes some disease</u>	→ <u>Turn off DNA in virus to kill disease</u>

1. D   2. D   3. B   4. A
5. B   6. C

Check-up

Page 36

A

1. D   2. D

B

1. genes   2. toxins   3. genome
4. bio-fuels   5. Chromosomes   6. fill out
7. junior   8. field
9. anonymous   10. prearrange

Answer Key

[Unit 4]

Conversation

Pages 38–39

A
1. A   2. B

B

Woman - Student	Man - Professor

• Needs advice on <u>how to interview</u>
• This is her <u>first time</u>
• <u>Thinks it sounds intense</u>
• <u>Is confident in her comprehension but is nervous about asking questions</u>
	• It can be <u>intimidating the first time</u>
	• The tips he gives her are:
	  - Have a good <u>attitude</u>
	  - Make sure people <u>can understand your questions</u>
	  - <u>Be prepared with a survey but must get consent</u>
	  - <u>Have a good comprehension of the material</u>

C
1. B   2. A   3. B

D
1. survey   2. consent   3. participate
4. comprehension   5. intense

Page 40

Woman - Student	Man - Professor
• Not looking forward to doing <u>interviews</u> • It is intimidating to <u>ask questions to people she doesn't know</u> • Asks if there are any other <u>options and if she can mail surveys to people</u>	• The more you practice, <u>the easier it gets</u> • Should have good comprehension <u>of the material and a good attitude</u> • <u>Wants students to do interviews because it is a class about communication styles</u> • <u>If unable to find people to interview then he will help</u> • <u>She has until the end of the semester, which is two months away</u>

1. B   2. D   3. C   4. A

Lecture

Pages 42–43

A
1. B   2. A   3. A   4. B

B and C
Underlined answers from part B.

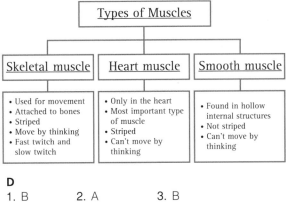

D
1. B   2. A   3. B

E
1. implies   2. internal   3. interval
4. alternating   5. Nevertheless

Pages 44–45

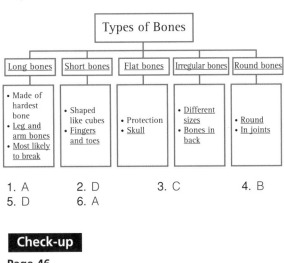

1. A   2. D   3. C   4. B
5. D   6. A

Check-up

Page 46

A
1. D   2. B

B
1. skeletal   2. smooth   3. striped
4. twitch   5. muscles   6. gather
7. especially   8. prepared
9. intimidating   10. tips

[Unit 5]

Conversation

Pages 48-49

A
1. B   2. A

B

Man - Student	Woman - University Worker
• Will graduate <u>at the end of the semester</u> • Looking for <u>career advice on what to do next</u> • Would like to be <u>a chef in the future</u> • <u>Wants to work in a restaurant</u> • <u>Is hard-working, honest, disciplined and works well under pressure</u> • <u>Specializes in making pastries and cakes</u>	• Assumes <u>that he is looking for catering work</u> • Will look for <u>face-to-face interviews for him</u> • Says it would be <u>beneficial to start looking for work now</u> • <u>Will take notes to give to potential employers</u> • <u>Will contact some businesses for the student</u>

C
1. B   2. A   3. A

D
1. face-to-face   2. graduate   3. categorize
4. passionate   5. afterward

Page 50

Woman - Student	Man - University Employee
• Looking for <u>a work placement for the summer</u> • Is a <u>first year student studying biology</u> • <u>Would like to get some experience in biology</u> • <u>Worked in catering for 3 months</u> • <u>Worried about her lack of experience</u>	• Students should <u>make appointments at the office</u> • Hard to <u>find work in biology</u> • <u>Asks for prior experience</u> • <u>Thinks she is passionate about biology</u> • <u>If she is disciplined she will do well</u> • <u>Will look out for placements</u> • <u>Career office is available before and after graduation</u>

1. C   2. B   3. C   4. A

Lecture

Pages 52-53

A
1. A   2. B   3. A   4. C

B and C
Underlined answers from part B.

How to Trade Stocks Successfully

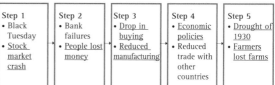

Step 1	Step 2	Step 3
<u>Decide on your goals</u> • Take a chance and make/lose money quickly • Or play it safe and make/lose money over a long time	<u>Assess the market</u> • Learn about different companies • Pencil trade and chart how you do	• <u>Find a stock broker</u> that you feel comfortable with and gives you advice • Buy some stocks

D
1. B   2. A   3. A

E
1. depression   2. Historically   3. ignorant
4. chart   5. industrialized

Pages 54-55

Steps that led to the Great Depression

Step 1	Step 2	Step 3	Step 4	Step 5
• Black Tuesday • <u>Stock market crash</u>	• Bank failures • <u>People lost money</u>	• <u>Drop in buying</u> • <u>Reduced manufacturing</u>	• <u>Economic policies</u> • Reduced trade with other countries	• <u>Drought of 1930</u> • <u>Farmers lost farms</u>

1. B   2. A   3. C   4. D
5. D   6. Yes, Yes, No, Yes

Check-up

Page 56

A
1. C   2. D

B
1. broker   2. share   3. stocks
4. stock market   5. trade   6. catering
7. specialize   8. placement
9. disciplined   10. appointment

[Unit 6]

Conversation

Pages 58–59

A
1. A   2. A

B

Man - Student	Woman - University Employee
• Would like to order a cheeseburger • Wants to know why the menu plan has changed • Thinks it is not rational • Is an active and healthy student • Thinks the school board should not be able to decide what he can eat • Is not happy that the change was involuntary	• School canteen will no longer serve junk food • School board cannot advocate an unhealthy diet • Thinks the board overreacted to worries about nutrition • Changes to the menu are made at the school board's discretion • Students should give the new healthy menu a try • There are many nice new dishes

C
1. B   2. Yes, Yes, No, No   3. A

D
1. advocate   2. discretion   3. behalf
4. arbitrary   5. rational

Page 60

Woman - Student	Man - University Employee
• Would like a recommendation on what to have for lunch • Friends usually order on her behalf • Would like the lasagna with salad • Is trying to avoid junk food • Cafeteria policy sounds outdated • Customers should be able to order what they want • Understands options are limited	• Recommends lasagna with French fries • Only available served with French fries • Policy of cafeteria to serve set dishes only • The decision is not arbitrary • Easier to monitor what is sold and to make orders that way • Will give the student a little salad this time

1. B   2. D
3. B   4. Yes, No, Yes, No

Lecture

Pages 62–63

A
1. A   2. A   3. B   4. C

B and C
Underlined answers are from part B.

The Influence US Entertainment Has on Other Countries

Cause		Effect
US entertainment	→	Imitation Leads to imitation in other countries
US entertainment, racially diverse	→	Racial understanding Helps people understand other cultures
US entertainment seen overseas, poor quality	→	Exposure to poor quality Leads to negative opinions of US entertainment
US entertainment shows Americans in a negative way	→	Negative opinions of Americans

D
1. B   2. A   3. A

E
1. street fashion   2. imitations   3. Dishonest
4. pop culture   5. Racial

Pages 64–65

Breakdancing

Cause		Effect
Breakdancing in US music videos	→	Breakdancing became popular in Korea
Popularity of breakdancing	→	Dance, musicals, and contests in Korea
Korean dance contests and popularity	→	Keeping breakdancing alive

1. D   2. B   3. C   4. D
5. A   6. A

Check-up

Page 66

A

1. A 2. B

B

1. encounter 2. discrimination 3. bias
4. dominant 5. ethnic 6. junk food
7. outdated 8. nutrition
9. involuntary 10. obesity

[Review 1]

Conversation 1

Page 67

Woman - Professor	Man - Student
• Says student hasn't <u>attended classes for the last couple of weeks</u>. • Asks if <u>everything is OK</u>. • Is sorry to hear about <u>grandmother</u>. • Says last week, they <u>reviewed material for the mid-semester</u> exam. • Likes to <u>consult with classes before she confirms exam</u>. • <u>Let class have some input into content of exam</u>. • <u>Asks if student studied while at home</u>. • <u>Says to graduate on time he must pass this course</u>. • <u>Has highlighted some of the more important areas</u>. • <u>Estimates student has about ten hours of study ahead</u>.	• Grandmother <u>died</u> so went home for <u>a week</u>. • Then, <u>got sick</u>, so stayed home for <u>a second week</u>. • <u>Wants to know if he missed a lot of work</u>. • <u>Says he didn't study while at home because he didn't take many books because didn't know he'd be gone so long</u>. • <u>Asks if professor has any handouts</u>. • <u>Has told boss he can't work this week because he plans to focus on studying</u>.

1. C 2. D 3. A 4. B

Lecture 1

Pages 68–69

Art movements of the early twentieth century

Fauvism
• <u>intense colors</u>
• <u>wild brush strokes</u>
• <u>think for themselves</u>

Cubism
• bits of the picture
• <u>bits put together out of place</u>
• <u>influenced by African and Native American art</u>

Expressionism
• <u>distorts reality to show feelings</u>
• <u>colors unnatural</u>
• <u>shapes exaggerated</u>

Futurism
• wanted to rebel
• <u>sought to be original</u>
• <u>glorifies war, violence, and patriotism</u>

1. B 2. C 3. B 4. C
5. C 6. True, True, False, True, False

Lecture 2

Pages 70–71

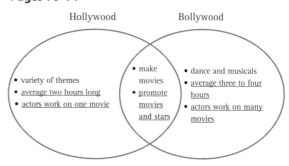

Hollywood
• variety of themes
• <u>average two hours long</u>
• <u>actors work on one movie</u>

(overlap)
• make movies
• <u>promote movies and stars</u>

Bollywood
• dance and musicals
• <u>average three to four hours</u>
• <u>actors work on many movies</u>

1. B 2. B 3. A 4. C
5. C 6. False, True, True, True, False

Lecture 3

Pages 72–73

Problem	Solution
<u>Losing fresh water supply</u>	→ <u>Don't waste water</u>
<u>Fresh water runs into the ocean and becomes salt water</u>	→ Protect vegetation and green space

1. B 2. C 3. A 4. C
5. B 6. False, True, True, False, True

Conversation 2

Pages 74

Woman - Student	Man - Librarian
• Looking for a <u>journal article</u> • Says she can't <u>see it</u> • Says doing well in assignment is <u>important</u> • Says she <u>needs the journal today or tomorrow</u> • <u>Says her paper is due on Monday at 5 o'clock</u> • <u>Asks what she can do</u> • <u>Says she's desperate, so will pay anything</u> • <u>Says thank you</u>	• Asks if the student <u>looked on the computer</u> • Says they should <u>look together</u> • Agrees it's not there • Says the student can <u>order the journal from another library</u> • <u>It could take up to one week to arrive</u> • Asks when <u>the student needs the journal by</u> • <u>Says the journal is unlikely to arrive before Monday</u> • <u>Asks if that is when the student's paper is due</u> • <u>Says he could call around and have one sent via express post</u> • <u>Will cost some money</u> • <u>Needs student to sign something to give her consent</u>

1. D 2. C 3. A 4. C

I Answer Key I **37**

Answer Key

[Unit 7]

Conversation

Pages 76–77

A

1. A   2. A

B

Woman - Student	Man - University Employee
• Removed the battery from her smoke detector	• In charge of checking that all the dorms have working smoke detectors
• Smokes in her dorm room	
• Doesn't like to go out in bad weather or when it is cold	• Has a master key for the rooms
• Didn't want to set off the smoke detector	• Dorm policy forbids smoking in any room on campus
• Said she was incredibly careful about smoking	• Makes the rooms smell bad for future residents
• Promises not to smoke in her room again	• Culprits can be expelled from the dorms
	• Won't mention it this time

C

1. A   2. A   3. B

D

1. forbid   2. genuine   3. incredible
4. indiscretion   5. explicit

Page 78

Woman - University Employee	Man - Student
• Had complaints about students cooking in their dorm rooms	• English is not very good
	• Forgot to clean his saucepan before class in the morning
• Student was listed as one of the culprits	• Has been cooking in his room
• Dirty pots can attract bugs and rats	• Was going to clean his pot after class
• Dorm contract forbids any cooking in dorm rooms	• Thinks the cafeteria food is very bad
• It could start a fire in the dorms	• Says he will not cook in the room again
• Will evict the student if it happens again	

1. C   2. C   3. D   4. A

Lecture

Pages 80–81

A

1. B   2. A   3. A   4. C

B and C

Underlined answers from part B.

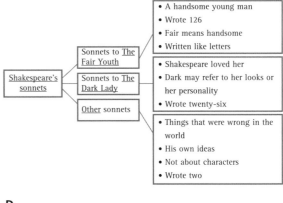

D

1. B   2. A   3. D

E

1. coherent   2. aesthetics   3. clarity
4. contradiction   5. appendix

Pages 82–83

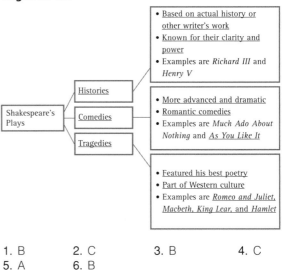

1. B   2. C   3. B   4. C
5. A   6. B

Check-up

Page 84

A

1. A   2. C

B
1. familiar   2. classified   3. sonnets
4. argument   5. listing   6. batteries
7. master key   8. culprit
9. smoke detector   10. in charge of

[Unit 8]

Conversation

Pages 86–87

A
1. B   2. A

B

Woman - Student	Man - Newspaper Editor
• Would like to <u>apply for a job at the student newspaper</u> • Is a <u>second year journalism student</u> • Hopes to get <u>some practical experience at the paper</u> • Thinks the paper <u>is famous and known for thorough research</u> • Is excited to <u>write articles that appeal to minorities and the masses</u>	• Is <u>the editor of the newspaper</u> • Says there are <u>still positions available</u> • Says the paper aims <u>to unify all the students at the school</u> • Says the paper tries to <u>be liberal in its views and appeal to everyone</u> • Says she must avoid <u>writing a distortion of the truth</u> • Wants the <u>student to write a few passages</u>

C
1. A   2. B   3. B

D
1. minority   2. ambiguous   3. distortion
4. unify   5. liberal

Page 88

Man - Student	Woman - Newspaper Editor
• Has an <u>article to submit for the newspaper</u> • Wrote about <u>the good and bad legacy of the dean of the school</u> • <u>Thinks the article has merit and should be shown to students</u> • <u>Reports about the dean's policy to change the ratio of ethnic minority students</u> • <u>Thinks it is morally ambiguous</u> • <u>Believes the story is balanced</u>	• Thinks <u>the story is interesting but will cause trouble</u> • Says the dean was <u>able to unify staff and students at the school</u> • <u>Says the dean improved the reputation of the school</u> • <u>Says the student should be careful not to write without evidence</u> • <u>Says the article praises the dean also</u> • <u>Says if the student makes some changes she will publish the story</u>

1. A   2. C   3. B   4. B

Lecture

Pages 90–91

A
1. B   2. A   3. B   4. A

B and C
Underlined answers from part B.

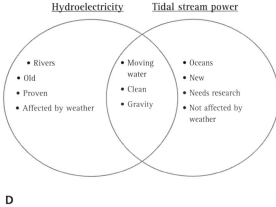

Hydroelectricity   Tidal stream power

• Rivers
• Old
• Proven
• Affected by weather

• Moving water
• Clean
• Gravity

• Oceans
• New
• Needs research
• Not affected by weather

D
1. A   2. A   3. B

E
1. annual   2. convert   3. volume
4. substitution   5. contrast

ges 92–93

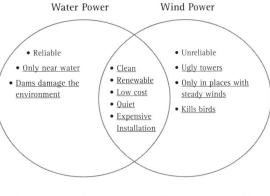

Water Power   Wind Power

• Reliable
• <u>Only near water</u>
• <u>Dams damage the environment</u>

• <u>Clean</u>
• <u>Renewable</u>
• <u>Low cost</u>
• Quiet
• Expensive Installation

• Unreliable
• <u>Ugly towers</u>
• <u>Only in places with steady winds</u>
• <u>Kills birds</u>

1. C   2. D   3. B   4. B
5. C   6. A

Check-up

Page 94

A
1. B   2. D

B

1. Hydroelectricity   2. proven   3. gravity
4. dam   5. drought   6. strive
7. article   8. legacy
9. edition   10. merit

[Unit 9]

Conversation

Pages 96–97

A

1. A   2. B

B

Man - Student	Woman - Professor
• Is going for <u>feedback on a thesis he wrote</u> • Has been <u>worrying about it all week</u> • Wrote about <u>how advertising works</u> • <u>Had trouble writing down some ideas clearly</u> • <u>Ran out of time toward the deadline</u>	• Thought the thesis was <u>quite good</u> • Noticed a few <u>problems that needed to be addressed</u> • Says most ideas were <u>concise and showed insight</u> • <u>Says it is important to back up everything</u> • <u>Says there were a few grammar and spelling mistakes</u> • <u>Says overall a good thesis that got a B+</u>

C

1. A   2. A   3. B

D

1. assessment   2. insights   3. thesis
4. demonstrate   5. concise

Pages 98

Woman - Student	Man - Professor
• Has finished <u>first draft of her history essay</u> • Would like <u>feedback</u> • Has done a lot of <u>research</u> • <u>Spent a long time, carefully writing it</u> • <u>Is proud of her paper</u> • <u>Will make the changes the professor recommends</u>	• <u>Says it is not always good to complete an assessment too quickly</u> • <u>Says the student has followed the given directions</u> • <u>Says the student has linked together evidence with her ideas</u> • <u>Says the student occasionally loses place and is side-tracked</u> • <u>Says the paper is concise and well written</u> • <u>Says if her thesis is the same it will be very good</u>

1. C   2. A   3. D   4. B

Lecture

Pages 100–101

A

1. A   2. A   3. A   4. C

B and C

Underlined answers from part B.

Theory	Evidence
<u>Psychoanalysis</u>: Behavior is the result of internal thoughts	→ People have thoughts they can't explain
<u>Behaviorism</u>: Behavior is the result of reward and punishment	→ People study hard to get good grades
<u>Humanism</u>: Behavior is the result of values and choices	→ Most people don't steal because it is wrong
<u>Cognitive</u>: Behavior is the result of reasoning and thinking	→ We have opinions about ourselves

D

1. A   2. B   3. A

E

1. ideology   2. intelligence   3. Depression
4. cognitive   5. overlapped

Pages 102–103

Problem	Solution
Damaged brain	→ <u>Neuro-chip restores cognitive abilities</u>
Damaged nerves in back (<u>can't walk</u>)	→ <u>Neuro-chip sends messages from brain (can walk again)</u>
<u>Depression</u>	→ Neuro-chip placed in brain to make parts work better

1. C   2. B   3. B   4. C
5. B   6. C

Check-up

Page 104

A

1. A   2. B

B

1. Behaviorism   2. schools   3. Psychoanalysis
4. reasoning   5. value   6. admit
7. address   8. Occasionally
9. relieved   10. feedback

[Unit 10]

Conversation

Pages 106–107

A
1. B   2. A

B

Man - Student	Woman - Professor
• Is worried <u>about his low grades in class</u> • Asks if <u>there is anything he can do to get extra credit</u> • Has had <u>some problems at home but they are over now</u> • <u>Would like to find a job or do an assignment for credit</u> • <u>Accepts the professor's offer</u>	• Has a <u>meeting at the Publishing Organization later</u> • Says the student has <u>begun to lag behind other students</u> • Is glad that <u>he has realized this before it is too late to get extra credit</u> • <u>Could assign him extra work or find him practical experience</u> • <u>Is writing a paper for the institute</u> • <u>Says the student could help with empirical research for credit</u>

C
1. A   2. B   3. A

D
1. empirical   2. scope   3. passive
4. intermediate   5. practitioner

Page 108

Woman - Student	Man - Professor
• Would like <u>an extra week to write a paper she is doing for extra credit</u> • Has <u>two other exams that week that she must study for</u> • <u>Could fall further behind if she has to do all three in one week</u> • <u>Has physics and chemistry exams</u> • <u>Is trying to better her grades</u> • <u>Promises not to make any more mistakes</u>	• Says that her request had better <u>be warranted</u> • Understands that <u>the student can't do extra work every week</u> • <u>Needs more notice for extensions</u> • <u>Says student has been too passive in trying to get extra credit</u> • <u>Says student will not get a job if she is always distracted</u> • <u>Gives the student one more chance</u>

1. C   2. A   3. B   4. C

Lecture

Pages 110–111

A
1. A   2. B   3. A   4. A

B and C
Underlined answers from part B.

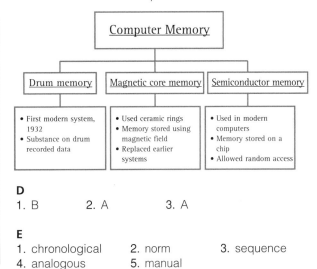

D
1. B   2. A   3. A

E
1. chronological   2. norm   3. sequence
4. analogous   5. manual

Pages 112–113

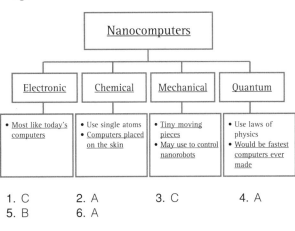

1. C   2. A   3. C   4. A
5. B   6. A

Check-up

Page 114

A
1. A   2. A

B
1. magnetic   2. obsolete   3. semiconductor
4. drum   5. ceramic   6. distracted
7. slight   8. warranted
9. lag   10. deficit

Answer Key

[Unit 11]

Conversation

Pages 116–117

A
1. A   2. A

B

Woman - Professor	Man - Student
• Her concern is <u>the student's research paper is very similar to one that is on the Internet</u> • Takes plagiarism <u>very seriously</u> • Says he copied <u>a lot</u> • <u>Says you must show that you are quoting</u> • <u>Says instruction on how to cite and the rules are in the handbook</u> • <u>Says he will get a failing grade and most likely suspension for at least four semesters</u>	• Used the Internet but <u>he didn't think he was plagiarizing</u> • Wants to take <u>a failing grade or delete the passages he used from the Internet</u>

C
1. B   2. B   3. A

D
1. suspension   2. quote   3. cite
4. repercussion   5. publication

Pages 118

Man - Student	Woman - Professor
• Is reading the <u>student handbook and has a question about plagiarism</u>	• Says all students could benefit from <u>reading the student handbook</u> • Is glad to know <u>someone is reading it</u> • Says plagiarism is <u>any thought or written work of another claimed by someone else</u> • <u>Says students can be suspended for 4 semesters</u> • <u>Says there is a writing center where he can have his work checked for plagiarism</u>

1. C   2. B   3. A   4. B

Lecture

Pages 120–121

A
1. A   2. B   3. A   4. C

B and C
Underlined answers from part B.

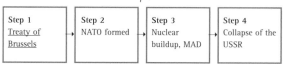

D
1. B   2. B   3. A

E
1. outcome   2. participation   3. Mutual
4. sought   5. albeit

Pages 122–123

1. B   2. B   3. B   4. B
5. C   6. C

Check-up

Page 124

A
1. C   2. D

B
1. assure   2. NATO   3. conventional
4. alliance   5. redefined   6. passage
7. plagiarize   8. handbook
9. instruction   10. degree

[Unit 12]

Conversation

Pages 126–127

A

1. A   2. B

B

Woman - Student	Man - University Employee
• Wants to talk about <u>the recreation area and change the snack bar hours</u> • Says the recreation area opens <u>at 7 and closes at 9 and the snack bar only opens on game days</u> • Wants the recreation facility open <u>until 10 and the snack bar open in the peak hours of the afternoon</u> • <u>Wants to see changes by end of spring semester</u>	• Is able to <u>arrange an appointment with the Site and Facility Committee</u> • Says they meet <u>twice monthly and beginning of next week</u>

C

1. A   2. A   3. B

D

1. site   2. valid   3. committee
4. commence   5. facility

Page 128

Woman - University Employee	Man - Student
• Heard <u>about the permission given to the student activities club to use the courtyard for concerts this spring</u> • Is interested in <u>becoming the sponsor of the club</u>	• Says it took a long <u>time to get the committee to agree</u> • Gave them <u>written proposal and valid reasons</u> • Was very <u>prepared</u> • Wants to host <u>5 concerts starting this spring</u> • <u>Needs a sponsor to be university employee representative at meetings twice a month</u>

1. B   2. B   3. B   4. C

Lecture

Pages 130–131

A

1. A   2. A   3. A   4. B

B and C

Underlined answers from part B.

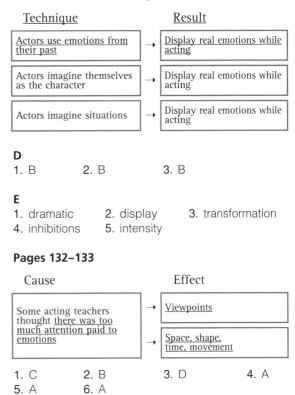

Technique		Result
<u>Actors use emotions from their past</u>	→	<u>Display real emotions while acting</u>
Actors imagine themselves as the character	→	Display real emotions while acting
Actors imagine situations	→	Display real emotions while acting

D

1. B   2. B   3. B

E

1. dramatic   2. display   3. transformation
4. inhibitions   5. intensity

Pages 132–133

Cause		Effect
Some acting teachers thought <u>there was too much attention paid to emotions</u>	→	<u>Viewpoints</u>
	→	<u>Space, shape, time, movement</u>

1. C   2. B   3. D   4. A
5. A   6. A

Check-up

Page 134

A

1. A   2. D

B

1. situation   2. approach   3. innocence
4. Method acting   5. scenes   6. in regards to
7. intramural   8. adjoining
9. peak   10. propose

Answer Key

[Review 2]

Conversation 1

Page 135

Woman - Student	Man - Professor
• Says she will graduate this year • Asks if professor can write her a letter of recommendation • Says she is applying to five programs • Hopes she will get into at least one • Gives professor forms to fill in • Says three of the programs are to do with liberal studies, but two of them are education programs • Says liberal studies is her major, but education is her minor. Thinks there is a lot of overlap between the two courses	• Says it would be his pleasure to write the letter of recommendation • Says it will be nice to write one where all his comments are genuine • Locates student's file • Asks what type of programs the student is applying to • Asks if they are all to do with liberal studies • Asks the student to give him a couple of days to complete the forms

1. C   2. D   3. A   4. B

Lecture 1

Page 136–137

```
        Things you can do to
          live a long life
```

Things you shouldn't do:	Things you should eat/drink:	Exercise:	Lifestyle:
• smoke • drink too much alcohol • eat processed foods • do dangerous things	• fruit and vegetables • fish • dark chocolate	• regular exercise	• regular sleep schedule • be optimistic • remain cognitively active • have friends

1. C   2. C   3. D   4. B
5. C   6. B

Lecture 2

Page 138–139

Step 1	Step 2	Step 3	Step 4	Step 5
The brothers listen to stories to study language	The brothers publish the stories	The stories become popular	The stories are translated into many languages	The stories are made into movies

1. B   2. C   3. B   4. C
5. B   6. False, True, True, False, True

Lecture 3

Page 140–141

Cause		Effect
rain and no flood control	→	floods
floods	→	hospitals and schools closed, many homeless people
100,000 homeless people	→	Red Cross evacuated people to safer areas
family members separated	→	Red Cross "family linking"
medical services needed teams	→	Red Cross set up medical centers and mobile medical teams
little or no food	→	Red Cross gave supplies

1. B   2. C   3. B   4. B
5. B   6. No, Yes, No, Yes, Yes

Conversation 2

Page 142

Man - Student	Woman - Financial Assistance Officer
• Says he needs to speak to someone about getting financial assistance • Asks if he has come to the right place • Says he is a student • Says he has gotten behind in rent, so needs a loan • Wants to borrow $300 • Has a part-time job, but doesn't know his annual income • Says he can pay it back in three months	• Asks if he is a student. If he is, he has come to the right place • They offer financial assistance to students, but not the general public • Asks how she can help • Says he might be eligible for an emergency student loan. Asks if she can ask a few questions • Asks how much he wants to borrow • Asks if he has a job and about his annual income • Asks how long it would take for him to pay back the loan • Says to be eligible for an emergency student loan need to: have a genuine and valid reason to apply, apply for less than $500, be employed, and be able to pay it back within six months

1. A   2. A   3. B   4. B